the spa lov

GUIDE TO EUROPE

Sarah Woods

NH
NEW
HOLLAND

Contents

Map of featured
spa lover's destinations

Numbers correspond to those listed on
Contents (*see pages 2–3*).

50 ICELAND

49 IRELAND

48 UNITED
KINGDOM

47

NETHERL

BEL

FRANCE

3

4

PORTUGAL   SPAIN

1

2

INTRODUCTION

Although the proliferation of swanky modern hotel treatment suites and urban wellness sanctuaries attempt to lay claim to the concept of spa therapies, 'health through water' (*sanus per aquam*, the Latin from which the 'SPA' acronym is thought to have derived) is far from being a new phenomenon or passing trend. Indeed the Mesopotamians, Egyptians, Minoans, Greeks, Romans (another school of thought is that the word 'spa' actually originates from the Latin verb *spagere*, meaning 'to pour forth') and later the Ottomans, Japanese and Western Europeans all used spas as a part of daily life.

Homer and other classical writers report that the Greeks indulged in a variety of social baths as early as 500 BC, including hot-air baths known as *laconica*. In 25 BC, Emperor Agrippa designed and created the first Roman *thermae* (a large-scale spa), and each subsequent emperor outdid his predecessor in creating ever-more extravagant *thermae*. In fact, large-scale organized spa facilities were an important part of life in the Roman Empire, as battle-weary legionnaires sought ways to encourage their bodies to recuperate effectively. The Romans were the first to look beyond the obvious – physical wounds, aches and fatigue – and consider the importance of emotional well-being as a part of wellness.

This holistic approach to the health of mind, body and soul was born out of the curative effects of natural thermal water. It soon became apparent that mineralized water sources were effective in healing ailments and could also ease stress and mental strain through relaxation. Building grand, ornate column-flanked bathing venues, the Romans actively promoted the positive health benefits of '*aquae*' and ingesting, inhaling and taking a dip in curative, all-natural waters. Over time, spa facilities evolved into full-blown social entertainment complexes where friends and workmates would gather to chat, debate, engage in sports, eat and relax. Many featured different types of baths containing waters of varying temperatures. Typically, the Romans would have enjoyed a physical workout before visiting a trio of progressively warmer rooms for a body bath, an exfoliation and a massage with oil anointment. Often, the ritual would involve a bracing dip in the ice-cold frigidarium.

The Spa Phenomenon

Water-based treatments became all the rage in the 4th century as the Romans conquered new territories and news of spa baths spread Europe-wide. Soon, variants of the Roman bathing rituals began to flourish as Greek and Turkish influences became wider known. Before long, steam therapies, balneology (hot and cold bathing using waters with different mineral compositions) and thalassotherapy (including seawater and natural marine

ABOVE *Blue Lagoon geothermal spa, near Reykjavik, Iceland.*

OPPOSITE *Calcite-rich waters in Pamukkale, Turkey.*

extracts, such as seaweed, algae, mud, salts and sands) attracted a medical following, as doctors championed the cause. Countries all over Europe began exploiting their natural spring-fed thermal sources for health purposes and by the mid-1800s a great many spa buildings and pump houses were built to better cater for the wealthy elite. Spa vacations became *en vogue* with the moneyed crowd of European aristocracy, royalty, nobility and landed gentry. Convalescence was so often the driving force behind a visit to one of Europe's most fashionable spa destinations during a time when disease continued to claim many lives.

Although saunas had began appearing along the Baltic as early as AD 1000, extreme heat, smoke and steam soon became inaugurated in a wider European spa-going tradition with sweating, freezing-cold plunges and a greater acceptance of nudity (and alcohol) embraced as health-giving in the Finnish tradition. Other influences included the hammam ritual, popularized by the Ottomans who built grandiose, domed and handsomely tiled cleansing venues complete with steam

rooms, private washing quarters and mosaic-clad massage suites together with social areas.

Soon, towns such as Germany's Baden-Baden, Czechoslovakia's Karlovy Vary and Bath in England (promoted as 'the premier resort of frivolity and fashion') were the 'in places' to 'take the waters'. By the late 19th century, Father Sebastian Kneipp had developed a holistic herbal and water therapy that was to become a cornerstone of the European spa industry. Born in 1821 in Bavaria in Germany, the son of a poor weaver, Sebastian Kneipp was studying for the priesthood when he was struck down with pulmonary tuberculosis – at that time a fatal disease with only one prognosis, death. However, by following a regime of hydrotherapy, involving short full-immersion dips in the icy waters of the River Danube, Kneipp made a full recovery. He founded the naturopathic movement and developed a form of hydrotherapy that focused on the application of water at various temperatures and pressures through different methods. Kneipp became the first proponent of a holistic system healing that rested on five main tenets:

- Hydrotherapy (water-based treatments)
- Herbalism (use of natural botanical medicines)
- Exercise (physical activity)
- Nutrition (a diet of wholesome grains, fruits and vegetables with limited meat)
- Spirituality (Kneipp believed that a healthy mind led to a healthy body)

As Popular as Ever

By the mid-20th century, the principles of Kneipp (in whole or in part) had filtered into many aspects of treatment for improved health and vitality – from weight loss and longevity to disease prevention and anti-stress relaxation. Many retained a strong clinical, medical focus that addressed the physical more than the spiritual (since July 2007, the number of medical spas has grown by 85 per cent, according to International Spa Association figures, proof that this type of spa is a force to be reckoned with in an era of modern medicine). Other spas developed with pampering to the fore, or concentrated on programmes of activity in the fresh air and diet. Today, the spa aesthetic – in all its many varied guises – has emerged as a strong element of popular culture, influencing everything from clothing, music and cosmetics, to architecture, home decor and cuisine. However, hydrotherapy – water – remains a core feature, either in the therapies and spa philosophies or in the harmonizing design of the spa venue: many centre on lotus ponds, fountains, water features and cascading pools in homage to this powerful natural healing force.

The number of spas continues to grow at around 20 per cent per annum – a phenomenal growth that has shown little sign of slowing down for almost a decade. Today a staggering array of spas caters for every possible ailment, beautification desire and style preference – from funky, urban day spas and beach-side resort spas to treetop forest spas, lake-front spas and alpine spas with a medical speciality, be it heart disease, high blood pressure, obesity or osteoporosis. As we adapt to cope with the greater stresses of modern life, we are seeking out ways to live longer, happier, healthier, more fulfilled and balanced lives. We recognize the need for pampering and pleasure as a right not a luxury. We understand that rejuvenation and the healing of mind, body and spirit go hand in hand with physical well-being. Even in a time of global economic downturn, spas continue to report an increase in visitors – proof that we view our physical and mental health as a priority and consider it a worthy investment, not a passing fad.

Modern Need for Spas

Three mega-trends are cited as the dynamos behind the continued surge in the wellness sector: an ageing world population; a move away from reliance on conventional medicine; and the powerful reach of celebrity wellness advocates. With over 285 million active wellness consumers in the world's top 30 industrialized nations alone, spas are responding to a growing demand for preventative programmes that improve overall quality of life (over 81 per cent of spa-goers want more than pampering). Despite huge medical advancements and technological and societal changes, today's spa sector is, in many ways, fulfilling the same role in wellness tourism as it did in the 1800s. Millions of spa-goers are travelling to destinations where they can pursue holistic, preventive or lifestyle-based activities to the benefit of their health.

However, today the sector is valued globally at more than $106 billion with more and more wellness centres and spas offering a greater degree of sophistication and individuality. Europe's 2,000 or so spas boast almost 200 million bed-nights, with the average spa-goer staying for around six nights, representing a major segment of the travel and tourism industry.

In this book I am going to guide you through the maze of European wellness options, focusing on natural spas (spas that have natural thermal waters) and destinations with long wellness histories (for example the use of local plants or mud within therapies). I present a range of destinations and treatments – from the sediment-rich curative mud wraps of Hungary's Lake Balaton region to the centuries-old water-based health traditions of the Czech Republic; from caviar facials in St Petersburg to Finland's oldest active public sauna. Some of the destinations you could certainly guess, I'm sure, but I've thrown a few surprises in, offering some suggestions that are off the spa-goers' beaten track.

Each entry details the history of the place, suggestions as to spas and therapies that you might want to try, contact details and pricing information and also suggestions as to other activities and attractions in the area.

BELOW Kaiser-Friedrich-Therme, Wiesbaden, Germany.

SPAIN

travel essentials

TIME ZONE: GMT +1

TELEPHONE CODE: +34

CURRENCY: Euro

CAPITAL: Madrid

LANGUAGE: Spanish

WHEN TO GO: Spain is generally divided into a temperate north and a hot, dry south, with April to October the most popular time to visit. In the height of summer (July and August) temperatures soar to scorching highs inland. Coastal regions remain pleasant year-round but are prone to wet weather in winter.

Inland Andalucía

The Moors left an outstanding legacy behind them in rural Al-Andalus (Andalucía) that reaches far out into all aspects of culture, architecture and health and wellness traditions.

ABOVE Saltwater bath, Aire de Sevilla.

OPPOSITE Moorish splendour of the Aire de Sevilla.

PREVIOUS PAGE View on Alhambra at sunset, Granada.

In the beautiful Andalucían village of Zújar, around 100 km (62 miles) from Granada City, the ancient thermal waters of this Moorish settlement have been renowned for their health-boosting qualities for several centuries. The village, which clings to the slopes of the Jabalcón Mountain, is flanked by spring-carved rainwater channels that plunge from the 1,496-m (4,908-ft) summit to the riverbed of the Guadiana Menor and the Negratín Reservoir below. The **Baños de Zújar**'s traditional bathing pool is filled year-round with healing natural thermal water (18°C/64°F) that the local people swear keeps them supple, hale and hearty (it is said to be especially beneficial for soothing arthritis pain). Used as a regular source of well-being (open seven days a week during August and Tuesday to Sunday every week of the year), these therapeutic waters offer unbeatable views across the striking Negratín Reservoir – and beyond.

Spicy Oils and Arabic Bathing

An elegant bathing temple can be found in the heart of the history-rich Santa Cruz neighbourhood in Seville, built on an old Moorish structure with Roman traces. Once public baths, the **Aire de Sevilla** has a trio of traditional Arabic bathing pools – a tepidarium (36°C/97°F), a caldarium (40°C/104°F) and a frigidarium (16°C/61°F) – together with some Moorish-influenced therapies.

Around 6km (3¾ miles) from Seville's city centre, a cup of refreshing fruit tea (from a charming Moorish-style *tetería*) welcomes visitors to the **Medina Aljarafe Baños Arabes** in the town of Bormujos. This Islamic hospitality tradition dates back to time immemorial and here customs and conventions take pride of place. Great care is taken to equalize the physical and mental balance in olden Moorish medicine, and to step into this tranquil haven is to forget the hectic pace of modern life. Blessed with an

3 things you **must not** miss

◀ **1 Mezquita, Córdoba**
Visit Córdoba's fine Mezquita (mosque), one of the largest in Europe, dating back to AD 600 and considered the most accomplished monument of Spain's Umayyad dynasty. *www.mezquitadecordoba.org*

2 Old Town, Cádiz
Immerse yourself in the late-night cubbyhole tapas joints and bars of Cádiz's historic Old Town, especially in the skinny backstreets that lead out from the Plaza de San Francisco. *www.cadizturismo.com*

3 Barrio Santa Cruz, Seville
Explore the colourful vibrancy of Seville's medieval quarter, Barrio Santa Cruz, a glorious old cityscape of plazas, wrought-iron gates, stone streets and patios filled with fountains and geraniums. *www.turismosevilla.org*

BAÑOS DE ZÚJAR

w www.altipla.com/zujar/
eng/presentacion.htm

*Entrance €2 adults / €1
children; open 10am–5pm
Tues–Sun in winter and
10am–7pm in the summer.*

AIRE DE SEVILLA

t + 34 955 010 025
w www.airedesevilla.com

*Relish the opulent Moorish
splendour of gold, burnt-red
and glazed tile-adorned
decor with flickering lamps.
Expect to pay €21 for a
standard bath and massage.*

MEDINA ALJARAFE
BAÑOS ARABES

t +34 954 788 344
w www.medinaaljarafe.com

*Bathe in cool, warm and
steam-shrouded hot water
before enjoying the peace
and quiet of the domed-
ceiling relaxation room,
from €40.*

HAMMAM SANCTI PETRI

t +34 956 016 903
w www.hammam
    sanctipetri.com

*Among echoing marble
bathing chambers lit by
Arabian lamps, try the
50-minute moisturizing
massage rich in herbal
essences, price from €65.*

*ABOVE The Giralda, the bell
tower of Seville Cathedral,
which can be seen from the
rooftop relaxation area of the
Aire de Sevilla.*

overriding sense of calm, the interior of the bathhouse is nuanced by moody lighting and soft Arabian melodies. Most guests opt for the great-value 100-minute bath package that includes a mild, hot and ice-cold dip, together with a whole-body massage and a steam bath. Whatever you choose, it is wise to reserve in advance as numerous diehards are daily bathers and the place can easily become fully booked.

Marbles, Mosaics and Moors

Located well away from the normal tourist haunts, the **Hammam Sancti Petri** in Chiclana de la Frontera is very much the domain of the serious traditional bathing aficionado. Under oh-so-opulent inlaid domed ceilings, Moorish lanterns and

grand, towering columns, the waters of Sancti Petri sparkle invitingly and are popular with large bathing groups of friends and family. Though a modern structure, considerable care has been taken to ensure this 1,800-sq m (19,375-sq ft) facility is every inch the homage to Arabic bathing 11th-century style. Using a mixture of authentic materials typical of the period, the Sancti Petri offers a journey back to the bygone age of Al-Andalus amid water pools, citrus-and-spice aromas and a mix of Greco-Roman-Islamic influences. Opt for a deluxe Salam body treatment for a full cleanse, scrub and sumptuous massage using richly nourishing heady perfumed oils and firm, kneading pressure to relieve muscular tension.

Costa del Sol

While the modern-day Costa del Sol is renowned throughout Spain for its glitzy five-star hotel spas and plush resorts, this squiggle of beach-scattered shoreline is rich in wellness history.

ABOVE *Finca Cortesin's aromatic steam room.*

An enthralling history-rich bathing venue can be found in the valley below Manilva, a couple of hours away from Ronda. The Roman-built sulphur baths of Hedionda sit on waters that flow from a limestone outcrop above the valley, providing a perfect spot for an arched bathing complex dating back 2,000 years. Frequented by Julius Caesar no less – the governor of southern Spain 63–60 BC – on account of the apparent curative properties of the sulphur-rich waters, **Los Baños Romanos de la Hedionda** soon became renowned as a place in which all manner of skin infections were healed. Remodelled by the Moors, the baths have been crudely restored in recent years in a style that blights the original majesty of the Roman structure. However, a stunning archway, tunnel and four chambers remain. So high is the sulphur and hydrogen content in these cool, murky waters that a strong aroma of rotten eggs is all-prevailing – a little off-putting to those used to more sterile bathing environments. Despite this, visitors enjoy a dip in Hedionda's 'brimstone brew' on a fine, lazy, sunny Sunday afternoon, overlooked by eucalyptus trees and crumbling Roman ruins on the banks of the Abarran Stream.

Beauty of Casares

The surrounding area of Casares is one of Andalucía's areas of outstanding beauty with national parks and Iberian-Phoenician settlements in among Arabic and Roman structures, including a fine castle. Its geographical location, between the mountainous range of the Serranía de Ronda, the Straits of Gibraltar and the coast, offers a striking diversity of landscapes punctuated by vineyards and whitewashed Andalucían villages with views out to sea. The spa at **Finca Cortesin**, on the hillside on the outskirts of the village of Casares, draws on aspects of the local

3 things you **must not** miss

1 Puerto Banús
Stroll along the cosmopolitan yacht-strewn waterfront at upscale Puerto Banús, where chichi boutiques and stylish cafes overlook gleaming million-dollar sailing craft. *www.puertojosebanus.es*

2 Traditional Village
Step back in time in charming whitewashed Ojén. Its steep, cobbled streets and quaint tapas bars are just a 10-minute drive (or bus ride) from super-swish Marbella. *www.ayto-ojen.es*

▶ **3 Museo Picasso, Málaga**
A visual feast of over 230 works by the great artist, donated by his family and compatriots. *www.museo picassomalaga.org*

ABOVE Bathe overlooking lush, palm-scattered gardens at Finca Cortesin.

OPPOSITE The Baños Arabes in Ronda are considered some of the best preserved Arabic baths in Europe.

cultural and wellness heritage. It blends Moorish pillars, fountains, palm trees and typically Arabic mosaics, lanterns and tables with twinkling tea lights in a decadent, upscale setting gloriously free from the pungent whiff of hydrogen sulphide. Here, among lush Mediterranean foliage, you'll find fluffy white robes, bowls of exotic fruit and readily available flutes of champagne. A sizeable menu of therapeutic and beauty treatments centres on the only Finnish snow cabin in Spain, together with several saunas, a steam room, Turkish bath and therapies that run from detoxifying seaweed wraps to numerous styles of massage using calm-inducing scented oils.

Mint Tea, Massage and Meditation

The **Agua de Oriente, Baños Árabes de Benalmádena** provide plenty of cultural references to a bygone time, in a handsome bathhouse inspired by 11th-century Moorish architecture. Offering visitors a traditional Spanish-Arabic bathing experience, with or without a traditional massage, the baths can be accessed in 90-minute slots. There are three pools – a tepidarium, a caldarium and a frigidarium – all decorated in grandiose Arabic style. Enjoy glasses of peppermint tea amid the aromas of citrus oils and spices.

Less than an hour away, the 11th-century Baños Arabes in the pretty whitewashed town of Ronda are well worth

INFORMATION

LOS BAÑOS ROMANOS DE LA HEDIONDA

w www.manilvalife.com/
   hedionda-and-the-roman-
   baths.htm

*Open year-round, pack
a swimming costume,
camera and towel.*

FINCA CORTESIN

t +34 952 937 800
w www.fincacortesin.com

*For the ultimate treat, book
a leisurely 80-minute
relaxation massage – a truly
sublime touch therapy that'll
take you to a blissful,
heavenly world of inner
calm (€110).*

AGUA DE ORIENTE, BAÑOS ÁRABES DE BENALMÁDENA

t +34 952 444 660
w www.aguadeoriente.com

*Breathe in pungent spicy
aromas to journey back in
time in baths inspired by
11th-century architecture,
where candlelit, oil-rich
massages are priced from
€37 for 30 minutes.*

BAÑO MÁGICO

t +34 952 212 327
w www.elhammam.com

*Choose traditional treatments
or opt for a fusion of Asian-
Mediterranean therapies that
blend lemon grass, ylang-
ylang, olive oil and geranium,
from €45.*

a visit, even though the waters are no longer accessible. Follow a set of rustic steps wedged into a rocky canyon, which lead from the Puente Viejo (Old Bridge) below the Salvatierra Palacio up to the bathing house. Here, classical musical concerts were once staged underneath domes peppered with star-shaped light and air vents. Used daily until the 17th century, Ronda's baths remain open for sightseers only. However, visitors can still swim in the waters of the Rio Guadalevin, where the Moors once purified themselves ahead of entering the baths.

In central Málaga, hidden among its many paved bird-scattered plazas and ancient backstreets, you'll find the **Baño Mágico** (Magic Bath), an authentic Moorish bath and traditional massage house. An oasis from the traffic noise of the city in Málaga's old Jewish Quarter, the bathhouse is in a charming 18th-century building. Sparsely furnished, there are curtained-off upstairs massage areas. The hottest hall (45°C/113°F) is the first port of call under a huge light-giving cupola. A series of cold- and hot-water sources, cleansing and exfoliation areas (therapies use the old-style soap and horsehair glove), showers and relaxation areas lead to the cold hall (16°C/61°F). Fountains adorn a contemporary Arabic chill-out room and meditation zone, while a Western-style dry hall – a recent addition – offers a range of massages, from Thai and shiatsu to Swedish.

FRANCE

travel essentials

TIME ZONE: GMT +1

TELEPHONE CODE: +33

CURRENCY: Euro

CAPITAL: Paris

LANGUAGE: French

WHEN TO GO: Coastal regions sizzle in July and August. Springtime and autumn are ideal seasons for hiking, cycling, climbing and running.

Vichy

As one of France's foremost spa towns, Vichy achieved considerable fame for its curative might when Napoleon III started taking its sulphurous waters in the 1860s.

Flocks of wellness tourists descended on this simple Auvergne settlement as word spread Europe-wide of Vichy's effectiveness in healing bodily aches and pains and digestive ills. But Vichy's history extends much further back than Napoleon III. Under the reign of Louis XIV, the town became a health resort of great elegance that was dubbed the 'second Paris'. However, Vichy's rich supply of mineralized waters first gained an international reputation during Roman times. The legions exploited the sulphur-laden beneficial virtues of the local springs during restorative bathing sessions.

Genteel Elegance

Today, Vichy is characterized by stately buildings that date from the 19th and 20th centuries, a reflection of the development of the town into a world-class spa resort. Although the grand old Thermal Establishment built in 1900 is now a beautifully converted upscale shopping mall, the elegant spa gardens, Parc des Sources, are still a central gathering point. The gardens have a handsome bandstand, in which genteel afternoon concerts take place, picnic areas and shaded spots in which people sit, read and chat. Visitors delight in these restful, green, public spaces before, or after, sampling Vichy's healing waters from the Célestin bronze taps on the Boulevard du President Kennedy, the source for the town's world-famous bottled spring water sold around the world.

Wellness Centres

Although Vichy suffers a little from its reputation as being a destination for a large number of affluent French pensioners, the town remains a fashionable wellness retreat.

In the cutting-edge 1990s-built **Thermes Callou**, 130 light and airy spa suites are fed by a mammoth pump room. Open

ABOVE Pressure-controlled water massage: the Vichy shower.

OPPOSITE Lavender and sunflowers in Provence (see page 24).

---

3 things you **must not** miss

1 Shopping Trip
Delve into Vichy's small boutiques, delicatessens and wine stores hidden among its riddle of old passages and pedestrian streets. *www.ville-vichy.fr*

2 Thrill of the Races
Visit l'Hippodrome, Vichy's lively horse-racing track (open May–September), which is host to a popular flat-racing festival in July. *www.courses-de-vichy.fr*

▶ **3 Night at the Opera**
Grab a ticket for one of the many outstanding ballets, orchestral concerts and musical performances at l'Opéra de Vichy, a stunning building notable for its Italian-style decor. *www.ville-vichy.fr/opera-vichy.htm*

INFORMATION

· · · · · · · · · · · · · · · · · ·

THERMES CALLOU
t + 33 4 70 97 39 60
w www.vichy-thermes-
callou-hotel.com

*A signature Vichy shower
is €45. This is a real treat
for spa-goers keen to soak
up the town's number-one
therapy.*

THERMES DES DÔMES
t + 33 4 70 97 39 60
w www.vichy-thermes-
domes-hotel.com

*Book online for three-night
spa breaks from €360 per
person, including breakfast
and signature treatments.*

April–December only, with accommodation in the adjoining Hôtel Ibis, the Callou specializes in one- to three-day spa breaks.

The sister centre, the **Thermes des Dômes**, is a more lavish affair, offering a wider range of individualized treatments that allows each guest to tailor-make their stay (accommodation is provided by the neighbouring Novotel Thermalia). Short health stays and wellness programmes centre on massage, fluorine-rich bathing and organic, nutrient-laden wraps. Water temperatures range from 22–45°C (72–113°F), with all six of the spring 'fresh- from-the-mountain' waters piped into the Hall des Sources (Hall of Springs) – Vichy's landmark spa building.

Both establishments have been awarded ISO 9002 certification by the Association Française pour l'Assurance Qualité (French Quality Assurance Association), a measure of the quality of the thermal spas at every level, from hygiene to hospitality. Using France's greatest concentration of thermal springs, the Thermes Callou and Thermes des Dômes have embraced the modern wellness ethos centred on the holistic balance of body, mind and soul.

RIGHT Taste spring water from the pump at the Hall des Sources pavilion.

OPPOSITE The sumptuous architecture and thermal fountains of the Thermes des Dômes.

Bordeaux

In 1999, in the prestigious wine-growing region of Bordeaux, the first vinotherapy wellness centre opened at the world-famous 18th-century Château Smith Haut Lafitte.

ABOVE Spa Vinothérapie®, Les Sources de Caudalie.

OPPOSITE Château Smith Haut Lafitte.

For centuries, the French have associated their national libation with good health, claiming that the secret to prolonging life is a good diet and turning a corkscrew. Apparently, the Romans doused themselves in wine in the name of beauty so the concept of so-called 'wine spas' is far from new. In the French court of King Louis XIV, the nobles also massaged their faces with grape skins to alleviate the signs of fatigue and leave their skin feeling soft, smoother and more toned. Today, the ancient health ethos of France translates into modern-day wine therapy, an array of sumptuous wine-soaked wellness rituals created to regenerate and rejuvenate mind, body and soul.

Wine-inspired Wellness
Blending modern winemaking techniques with age-old organic viniculture methods, the sumptuous **Spa Vinothérapie®** within Les Sources de Caudalie at Château Smith Haut Lafitte (located south of the city of Bordeaux, in Martillac) has over 35 wine-inspired lotions, potions, scrubs and tonics, including sumptuous oils created by husband-and-wife team Mathilde and Bertrand Thomas. At Spa Vinothérapie® wine lovers can revel in their passion thanks to a vinotherapy package that lavishes spa-goers with the finer things in life. Denial and deprivation are alien concepts here.

Under the motto 'Salus per vinium' (Healthy living through grapes), no part of the vine is wasted. Therapies utilize vines rich in nutrient-heavy polyphenols, and grape pulp, stalks and seeds that boast detoxifying, anti-ageing properties around 10,000 times stronger than vitamin E. Grapes contain an abundance of vitamins, minerals and elements in traces, including vitamins A and B-group, vitamins C and E, sodium, fluorine, magnesium, iron, potassium, calcium, phosphorus and fruit acids. Wine therapies at Spa Vinothérapie® use varietal wines and their extracts, grape

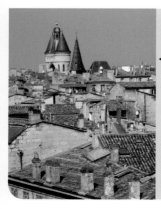

3 things you **must not** miss

◀ **1 Old Town, Bordeaux**
Take a leisurely meander through the history-rich, narrow, cobbled streets of Bordeaux's Old Town to the Quartier St Pierre's balconied buildings, wrought ironwork and charming plazas.
www.bordeaux-tourisme.com

2 Wine Country
Visit surrounding vineyards and wineries using a local wine map, available free from the Maison du Vin, 1 cours du XXX Juillet, Bordeaux.
www.vins-bordeaux.fr

3 River Cruise
Take an hour-long boat cruise up the river and all around Bordeaux's harbour, departing from the Quai des Chartrons year-round. For schedules contact the tourist office.
www.bordeaux-tourisme.com

juices, pressed (crushed) grapes and the remains of pressing, flour, bran and the cold-pressed oil from grape seeds. Bioactive substances from the grapes and wine are ultra-effective in cleansing, peeling, massage and bathing as well as in compressions, packs and face masks. Deep wrinkles are softened and milder lines retreat as the full 'pumping' effect of the stimulation of microcirculation and the production of collagen is experienced.

Softening, Soothing and Strengthening

Therapies promote metabolic boosting and the excretion of toxins from the connective tissue, thus making skin firmer, tighter and pinkish. Our skin naturally preserves moisture as its tissue strengthens and becomes more elastic, shedding dead and damaged cells and encouraging new skin cells to form. It is also believed that wine therapies can help to strengthen the immune system, act against cancer, improve lung function, promote healthier blood vessels, protect against stomach ulcers and stimulate the functions of the brain and nervous system.

Aside from the Bordeaux barrel baths, Merlot wraps and red-wine detoxifying teas, there are beautifully prepared meals in a Michelin-star restaurant accompanied by a vintage from a 13,000-bottle cellar. The selected menus are based on foods that foster vitality, health and beauty – and are wonderful to eat. Wine-tasting sessions ensure every aspect of the sophistication of the grape is truly relished for a real 'full-bodied' wine experience. *Santé*!

INFORMATION

SPA VINOTHÉRAPIE®, LES SOURCES DE CAUDALIE
t + 33 5 57 83 82 82
w www.sources-caudalie.com

The sublime half-day Vinothérapie® ritual including unlimited 100 per cent organic herbal teas, fresh grapes and use of steam rooms, relaxation rooms and thermal baths with massaging jet-stream is around €195.

Provence

As the most famous lavender-growing region on the planet, Provence has thousands of fragrant hectares of violet-blue tufts swaying in the warm Mediterranean breeze.

INFORMATION

LE COUVENT DES MINIMES HÔTEL & SPA
t +33 4 92 74 77 77
w www.couventdes
minimes-hotelspa.com

Check for seasonal spa offers, such as the two-night package including massage, facial, use of the indoor chromotherapy pool, sauna, laconium, caldarium and relaxation zone, with natural juice drinks and herbal teas. (Prices start at €540.)

FOUR SEASONS RESORT PROVENCE
t +33 4 94 39 90 00
w www.fourseasons.
com/provence

Feeling tense, stressed or anxious? Then opt for the calming 80-minute full-body massage, which involves unhurried strokes at medium pressure to soothe away tension and strain and unknot tightened muscles (€180).

ABOVE Lavender promotes relaxation.

RIGHT Pool, Four Seasons Resort Provence.

OPPOSITE Four Seasons Resort Provence.

Although lavender is recognized for its heady perfume, the healing properties of lavender were cherished as far back as 2,500 years ago when ancient Egyptians used it to help induce sleep. Roman soldiers scented the air with it to aid relaxation, and fields of hardy plants soon cropped up across Europe. In medieval and Renaissance Europe, monasteries added lavender to their medicinal herb gardens. Beloved by nobility and the aristocratic classes, lavender was used in a variety of forms by royalty. Lavender tea and jams were favourites of Queen Elizabeth I of England, while in France Louis XIV enjoyed lavender-scented baths and Charles VI demanded lavender-filled pillows. By the mid-19th century, lavender was considered a cure-all herb due to its therapeutic healing qualities and sweet-smelling naturopathic powers.

Stimulate the Senses

In Provence, lavender is the hallmark of the region's picturesque terrain, when in early summer the horizon fills with a dazzling display of indigo-blue-mauve hues.

An overwhelming natural scent dominates the warm, lazy breeze as the locals pick a few bunches to flavour herbal teas and scent their homes. Farmers harvest crops of lavender for organic oil for use in soap, face wash, shower gel, bath salts and hand and body lotion. As a herbal medicine, lavender is often used in natural spa therapies for its soothing, relaxing properties and calming effect. In aromatherapy massages, constituents of lavender oil can help to alleviate anxiety, insomnia, depression and hypertension. By adding a few drops to base oils, lavender can be massaged into the temples, shoulders or neck to aid the relief of tension headaches and ease away worries and stress.

Natural Wellness Traditions

At **Le Couvent des Minimes Hôtel & Spa**, Mane en Provence, a sumptuous range of wellness therapies focuses on indulgence and Mother Nature, marrying the scents and fresh produce of the Mediterranean – such as lavender, lemon, verbena, olives and honey – with the highest professional standards of French hospitality. This handsome spa stays loyal to the luxurious l'Occitane beauty and wellness brand and the natural well-being traditions of Provence.

Upscale l'Occitane has remained faithful to this landscape, where its products were conceived. Using only the finest lavender oils derived from freshly picked, locally grown flowers, the spa prides itself on delivering the ultimate luxury aromatherapy massage – unhurried, leisurely and with a strong connection to the natural landscape. Tucked away in the rolling hills of the picturesque Provençal countryside, this former convent dating from 1613 ensures spa-goers benefit from the utmost in quiescence and serenity. Mediterranean light and colours envelop this quaint boutique hotel and its peaceful spa, which is just a short drive from the French Alps to the north and Aix-en-Provence to the south.

Another lavish spa property can be found in the heartlands of lavender-scented Provençal meadows. In grand style, the **Four Seasons Resort Provence** at Terre Blanche is a temple to modern luxury blessed with space and calm. A 3,000-sq m (32,291-sq ft) spa housed in a two-storey ochre villa comes with a column-flanked black granite pool and has every conceivable luxury. For the ultimate in pampering that'll transport you to heaven try the decadent two-hour Provençal Escape, in which French olive oil infused with lavender buds is used. This is an ethereal delight.

3 things you **must not** miss

◀ 1 Musée de la Lavande
This museum in Coustellet outlines the historical importance of Provence's lavender industry, complete with video presentation, photographs and lots of sweet-smelling artefacts. *www.thelavendermuseum.com*

2 Canoeing
Canoeing on the scenic River Cèze offers some interesting rapids on a gentle stretch suitable for beginners and family groups. *www.ceze-canoe.com*

3 Caves, Aven d'Orgnac
These caves are worth a visit, with several huge chambers packed with stalagmites and stalactites. *www.orgnac.com*

ITALY

travel essentials

TIME ZONE: GMT +1

TELEPHONE CODE: +39

CURRENCY: Euro

CAPITAL: Rome

LANGUAGE: Italian

WHEN TO GO: Italy's temperate climate has regional variations. Summers in the south are extremely warm and sunny. The sea is warm enough to swim in from June to September.

Campania

Campania is renowned throughout Italy for its sun-blessed, curative climate, classical architecture and dramatic coastline, with the offshore bijou isle of Ischia a haven of natural spa therapies.

In this region some of Italy's wildest terrain surges with natural, primeval energy, with smouldering volcanic craters, knotted patchworks of aged olive groves, rock-studded cliffs and eerie lakes shrouded in ancient health myths. First discovered by recuperating Greeks and Romans, Italy's self-proclaimed 'therapeutic hub' is a rich source of health-giving natural properties, from sparkling lagoons of thermal mineral-rich seawater to deep-penetrating healing mud. Both the Greeks and Romans built several bathing venues in Campania to fully exploit the natural geological and hydrothermal phenomenon. Today these once-grandiose column-flanked complexes can be enjoyed as fine archaeological ruins. Beautifully preserved under volcanic water, ash and carbonized debris, you can visit the 'lost' city of Herculaneum, south-east of Naples, where you can view the Thermae (Roman Baths) and see the pools' original mosaics, washroom and lockers.

Magnetic, Steam and Volcanic Therapies

The island of Ischia offers more than its fair share of unrivalled spa delights. Renowned for its thermal gardens – a collection of hot natural pools within a park – Ischia has long been a place of tranquil relaxation where visitors can dip in and out of curative waters. A year-round pleasing climate and Ischia's nutrient-rich spring waters are very good reasons why the island is home to some of the best spas in Italy.

In the pretty Bay of Citara the island's very own Eden can be found in the **Giardini Termali Poseidon** (Poseidon Thermal Gardens) – Ischia's body and soul therapeutic retreat. Built in harmony with the natural surroundings, the garden's healing and beneficial powers are said to bring about a holistic feeling of balance and well-being. As a consequence, it is frequented by a wide range of visitors, from

ABOVE Mosaic at Herculaneum Thermae (Roman Baths).

OPPOSITE Gushing thermal jets and pools at Negombo Giardini Termali (Negombo Thermal Gardens).

PAGE 27 View of Capri.

3 things you **must not** miss

1 Caserta Vecchia
Vist the handsome Roman hamlet of Caserta Vecchia, at the foot of Mount Virgo, which was founded by the Lombards in the 8th century. *www.casertavecchia.net*

2 Mount Vesuvius
One of the smallest active volcanoes in the world, you can climb to the top along a steep gravel path. *www.parco nazionaledelvesuvio.it*

▶ **3 Palazzo dello Spagnolo**
This spectacular Naples palazzo is a stunning edifice, with grand staircases, archways and stuccoed transoms. *www.inaples.it*

**GIARDINI TERMALI
POSEIDON**

t + 39 081 908 71 11
w www.giardiniposeidon.it

*Lush gardens and easily
accessible thermal bathing
pools, fountains and walking
trails. Entrance fee €25–30
(spa therapies extra).*

**NEGOMBO GIARDINI
TERMALI**

t +39 081 98 61 52
w www.negombo.it

*Flower-filled parklands
containing a thermal bathing
venue. Entrance €30–35
(spa therapies extra).*

JKSPA

t +39 081 838 40 01
w www.jkcapri.com

*Enjoy top-of-the-range
pampering with poolside
views of softly rounded hills,
gorgeous sea panoramas
and sunsets. Budget for
€120 for a full-hour marine
algae body rub complete
with coarse-grain marine
nutrients.*

those suffering from chronic fatigue or attempting to slow the signs of ageing to people keen to address metabolic imbalances, stress and a variety of medical complaints. The locals swear the garden's thermal baths contain some of the most curative waters in Europe, due to their volcanic origins.

Various massages are offered either in the waters or in a therapy suite together with a range of therapies including volcanic mud masks for dermatological complaints.

Similarly, the **Negombo Giardini Termali** (Negombo Thermal Gardens) have long attracted wellness tourists looking for natural health solutions. Islanders believe the thermal springs here have been used since antiquity for the treatment of bodily aches, pains and fatigue because of their healing chemical properties and spectacular beach-front location.

Glitzy Capri

On Capri, the centres for well-being are a more sophisticated, modern affair yet also promote many of the ancient natural health philosophies. The **JKSPA** at the JK Place hotel is 100 per cent futuristic in design with its minimalist simplicity and sleek, uncluttered style. Though housed in a classic 19th-century building built on top of some Roman cisterns and a stretch of Roman road, the JKSPA is up-to-the-minute. Yet, beyond the ultra-swish modernity you'll find plenty of old-fashioned Italian hospitality and health ideas. The emphasis here is on opulence and a sumptuous range of decadent body wraps using mega-rich clay and mud and purifying herbs and marine algae ensures just that. Although, to the tension-wracked fresh arrivals the greatest luxury of all could just be the blissful peacefulness and jaw-dropping views out across the sea.

RIGHT Mineral-rich baths at the Giardini Termali Poseidon (Poseidon Thermal Gardens).

Lipari

The largest of a chain of seven islands in the UNESCO-protected volcanic archipelago that straddles the gap between Mount Vesuvius and Mount Etna, Lipari dates back to around 20,000 BC.

Lying about 30km (18½ miles) off the north-eastern coast of Sicily, the rugged volcanic terrain is still considered active, although the last recorded eruption occurred in the 5th century when a slew of airborne pumice deluged Roman villages on the island. Steaming fumaroles are still present on the island and hydrothermal activity causes hot, bubbling pools of mineral-heavy waters to form. Huge reserves of pale-grey pumice have long been the economic bedrock of Lipari. Under the Roman Empire, the rocks were used in the construction of the Pantheon's huge dome while the island was used as a bathing retreat (its hydrothermal waters are still used for baths today). Now, the pumice is harvested and shipped around the world to be used in wellness therapies. Few materials are as effective as an exfoliating skin softener, complexion enhancer, dermal cleanser, hair remover and buffer of dead skin layers, calluses and corns as pumice.

Beach and Bath

Stretching 10km (6 miles) at its longest point with a width of just 4km (2½ miles), Lipari is immortalized by postcard snaps of the creamy-alabaster waters of Spiaggia Bianca (White Beach), one of the most beautiful on the island and named for the sediments of pumice that have fallen into the sea over time. Close by, the Cave di Pomice di Porticello is a pale-water bay by a number of now-empty pumice quarries and workshops. Deposits of unwanted, extracted pumice now hardened by time form mounds along the shore – passing bathers simply help themselves to exfoliate in shallow waters, covered in white silt.

Pumice Treatments

Wellness therapies at the **Hotel Tritone Lipari** take place overlooking the sea and scenic Aeolian gardens. Many of the creams and cleansers contain crushed pumice stones to provide a gentle exfoliating agent

3 things you **must not** miss

1 Fresh Catch

Join the fishing folk on the harbourside in the early-morning sunshine to snap up the best of the daily catch, from squid and octopus to swordfish and mackerel.

2 Take a Boat Cruise

Seas that once carried ancient Greek traders and Roman warships are today the cruising ground of the rich, famous and fashionable in million-dollar yachts and schooners.
www.arcipelagoeolie.it

▶ 3 Escape on a Scooter

Explore the countryside with its rolling hills, awe-inspiring mountains, sandy coves, lemon groves and whitewashed villages. Visit the tourist information office at Corso Vittorio Emanuele, 202, for advice.

· · · · · · · · · · · · · · ·

HOTEL TRITONE LIPARI
t +39 090 981 15 95
w www.hoteltritone
lipari.com

Year-round special well-being packages offer an array of therapies such as the Weekend Wellness Break (from €515) including different massages, leisure and fitness activities and relaxation treatments.

ABOVE Sheltered bays and the fertile terrain of Lipari's ancient landscape.

on sensitive skin. Pumice is also evident in a range of luxurious pedicure and manicure treatments, loosening the cuticles and softening hardened soles. Used in conjunction with rich, nourishing emulsions, careful rubbing with a pumice stone in slow, circular movements can work wonders on dry, cracked rough skin – and can even remove those annoying wisps of unwanted toe hair by rapid, light movements back and forth. Natural handmade soaps composed of extra-virgin olive oil enriched with pure essential oils, flowers and volcanic lava are also used.

SWITZERLAND

travel essentials

TIME ZONE: GMT +1

TELEPHONE CODE: +41

CURRENCY: Swiss Franc

CAPITAL: Bern

LANGUAGES: German, French, Italian, Romansh

WHEN TO GO: Although renowned for its snowy, cold ski regions, Switzerland is blessed with over 290 days of sunshine and boasts warm summers when temperatures can rise to around 30°C (86°F). Even in the mountains the sun is hot, while winters rarely become cold enough to drop below -5°C (23°F), apart from on higher ground.

Arosa and Tarasp

A traditional form of Swiss bathing has experienced a renaissance, intriguing the modern wellness scene with its combination of two elements of Swiss culture – natural health and dairy farming.

ABOVE White daisies are just one of the many types of wildflower that grow in Swiss meadows.

OPPOSITE Pines, pure air and the natural mountain springs of Arosa.

PREVIOUS PAGE St Moritz (see page 37).

Today, taking an open-air Swiss *molke* (whey) bath in a wooden tub on a grass-topped Alpine peak has become all the rage – again. Taking a dip in this milky-white froth feels rather like being a modern Cleopatra. Wellness tourists are discovering that there is something wonderfully wholesome and nurturing about lying in a deep bath of milk next to an Alpine cheese hut as Switzerland's country folk did in times gone by. Popular in Switzerland's mountain regions, according to rural lore this dairy-rich immersion is believed to make the skin silky soft, help fight the signs of ageing and rejuvenate each and every cell and sinew in the body.

Whey-bath Experience
Generally, this is what a whey bath involves. After stripping off in a wild-flower meadow, you lower yourself gently into the bath to allow your body to absorb the soothing qualities of the whey. You relax into the milky depths to feel the positive effects of the liquid on the skin as it helps to regulate the skin's pH, stabilizes the acid barrier of the surface of the body, smoothes wrinkles and carefully cleans the outer dermal layers.

Heated to a temperature of around 38°C (100°F), the whey soon engulfs every bodily nook and cranny, helping to alleviate itchy skin and relieving allergies and improving the complexion. Freshly produced from working cheese farms, the whey comes straight from the cow to the tub. Around 30–40 minutes is the ultimate whey-bath wallow. The experience is enhanced by the surroundings – panoramic views of Alpine peaks and the smell of scented pine forests further stimulate the senses. Few scenes are as restorative as that of cattle on a backdrop of cut-glass peaks and the sound of tinkling cowbells and mooing herds.

Old-fashioned farming culture in Switzerland fiercely upholds traditions, and whey bathing is a lasting legacy of the

3 things you **must not** miss

◄ 1 Schloss Tarasp
Revel in the historic 11th-century grandeur of Tarasp's magnificent castle, perched on top of a pine-trimmed peak. *www.schloss-tarasp.ch*

2 Summer Music
During the summer Arosa hosts a number of musical events, including opera and musicals and a jazz festival. *www.arosa.ch*

3 Mountain Railroad
Experience jaw-dropping snow-topped vistas at a gloriously leisurely chug-chug pace on one of Arosa's charming mountain railroads. *www.arosa.ch*

INFORMATION

ALP LAISCH

t +41 78 708 25 31

w www.myswitzerland.com
(see below)

Pre-booking is essential, with prices from CHF 40 for a deep, whey-milk dip (check www.my switzerland.com/en/home/ autumn/excursion-summer/landscapes/scuol-tarasp-warm-whey-bath-with-a-view.html).

BERGOASE SPA, TSCHUGGEN GRAND HOTEL

t +41 81 378 99 99

w www.tschuggen.ch

A 20-minute whey bath costs CHF 70.

country's dairy-herding heritage. Spa-goers who give it a try swear that they feel revitalized and restored – and that can't be dismissed as the dizzying effects of altitude surely?

Where to Experience It

In historic Tarasp, on the River Inn, surrounded by glaciers and rugged peaks, the traditional Swiss whey bath is offered by a small, independent cheese-farmer at the **Alp Laisch** dairy on a one- or two-person-per-day basis. Set among scattered Alpine hamlets, a small lake and the towering spires of the Schloss Tarasp (castle), enjoying a nutrient-rich dip here allows wellness tourists to enjoy the warmth of

rural Swiss hospitality before a hike up to the mountain summits or a stroll around the 11th-century splendour of the castle.

Nestling in the snow-capped peaks of Arosa, the **Bergoase Spa** at the Tschuggen Grand Hotel (see page 36) is in a magnificent setting that is matched by the stunning design of the building's stylish interior. Created by Mario Botta and opened in 2006, the 5,000-sq m (53,819-sq ft) spa combines Alpine-evoking rugged white granite and polished maple. A dozen cosy therapy rooms offer a wide array of pampering, including a bath in whey from the resort's own Sennerei Maran Dairy. This is the option for you if the prospect of bathing outdoors doesn't appeal.

Graubünden

In recent years, the leafy valleys of Graubünden have grabbed the imagination of wellness tourists seeking something bold, exciting and new.

ABOVE *Snow trails of Diavolezza.*

OPPOSITE *Wonderful views from the Bergoase Spa.*

Here, a world away from traffic congestion, parking woes, tooting horns and spewing fumes, the ethos of tranquillity reigns supreme. Calming dips can be enjoyed in the sensual warm waters of spas in a wide variety of guises, from old-style bathhouse buildings and modern wellness centres to some of Europe's most stunning, sumptuously appointed architect-designed iconic landmark structures.

Restful Alpine Splendour

Set in the peaceful Schanfigg Valley at an altitude of around 1,800m (5,905ft) above sea level, Arosa benefits from an imposing mountainscape dominated by dramatic frosted peaks. A famous Alpine health resort since 1877 because of its pure air and sheltered, sunny location, Arosa is free from transit traffic and is accessible by the Swiss railroad from Chur or by car along 365 hairpin bends and through several mountain tunnels.

Arosa is home to the gorgeous, deluxe **Bergoase Spa** at the Tschuggen Grand Hotel (see page 35), designed by highly regarded Swiss architect Mario Botta. This spa is every inch the Alpine oasis. Built from white granite and rich, honeyed woods, this mountain paradise makes spectacular use of reflecting light and water. Splash around in the Arosa rock grotto, relax in the whirlpool or luxuriate in a high-tech sauna before cooling down after an afternoon on the sun terrace with a bracing ice shower and chill-out session. Choose therapies à la carte or opt for a short-stay package, such as the three-day H2O Deluxe in a private suite with sauna, steam bath and whirlpool.

Famous throughout Switzerland for its moonlight skiing in winter, the resort town of Diavolezza is reached by cable car at a height of 2,978m (9,770ft) from Val Bernina in the Bernina Pass Valley. With good snow conditions lasting well into May, Diavolezza is popular with Europe's skiing in-crowd,

3 things you **must not** miss

◀ 1 Glitz of St Moritz
Join the moneyed elite at horse racing and polo competitions on the scenic flower-trimmed shores of the beautiful Lake St Moritz. *www.engadin.stmoritz.ch/stmoritz*

2 Chur
This may be Switzerland's oldest city but it is host to lively cultural events and nightlife. Go on a walking tour of the historic Old Town. *www.churtourismus.ch*

3 Swiss Grand Canyon
Delve into Graubünden's Rhine Gorge for a spectacular hike with dramatic views along woodland and gorge trails. *www.graubuenden.ch*

INFORMATION

• • • • • • • • • • • • • • • • •

**BERGOASE SPA,
TSCHUGGEN GRAND
HOTEL**
t +41 81 378 99 99
w www.tschuggen.ch

*Prepare to be wowed by
an array of pampering
packages together with
a sizeable menu of 'pick
and mix' therapies, such
as an aroma oil massage
(CHF 140).*

BERGHAUS DIAVOLEZZA
t +41 81 839 39 00
w www.engadin.stmoritz.ch

*Take a break from gruelling
glacier hikes to relax in
Europe's highest-altitude
whirlpool bath (check
website for opening times).
CHF 25 for day guests,
including towel and robe.*

**MEDIZINISCHES
THERAPIEZENTRUM
HEILBAD ST MORITZ**
t +41 81 833 30 62
w www.heilbad-stmoritz.ch

*Drawing on aromatic Alpine
botanicals for its sumptuous
therapies, the herbal
massages are out of this
world (from CHF 98).*

THERME VALS
t +41 81 926 80 80
w www.therme-vals.ch

*An 80-minute exfoliation and
thalasso bath treatment at
this uber-stylish wellness
temple costs CHF 138.*

who revel in the gasp-inducing panorama of death-defying ravines, snow-capped peaks and rugged mountain trails. Off-piste, the **Berghaus Diavolezza** provides a sanctuary of relaxation and has the highest-altitude whirlpool bath in Europe, set at 3,000m (9,842ft) above sea level. Deep, warm waters offer heavenly respite for glacier hikers and mountain climbers who relish the Swiss-style rest and relaxation, complete with roaring fires and a restorative massage.

Holistic Mountain Pampering

After finding fame through its naturally healing carbonated mineral springs, the plush resort of St Moritz has established itself with Europe's well heeled as a firm fixture on the Swiss wellness circuit. The **Medizinisches Therapiezentrum Heilbad**

St Moritz draws on local curative elements, spa traditions and lots of medical know-how. Dozens of treatments centre on the resort's therapeutic waters, with others created using the area's nutrient-rich Alpine moor mud. For smooth, soft skin try the Alpine Herb Therapy – a tantalizing body treatment using local healing plants that helps to reactivate the metabolism, tones and cleanses, and balances pH levels. Active Alpine pursuits form a part of the spa's wellness ethos, with trails offering rugged hikes through stunning scenery.

The region's ultimate mountain wellness experience can be found at the chic, contemporary resort of **Therme Vals**, where natural thermal waters and eye-popping architecture make this undoubtedly Switzerland's most visually distinctive spa. This impressive masterpiece is an extraordinary cutting-edge design built from 60,000 layered pure quartz pieces with illuminated light effects. Greenish in colour, in order to fully harmonize with the mountain landscape, Therme Vals evokes a mystical, moody magnificence that is positively ethereal. This iconic structure is designated a protected monument and architect Peter Zumthor has won many awards for his unique design. Signature therapies utilize healing minerals in numerous different baths together with lymphatic massages and sensuous spring-water showers.

BELOW Ancient waters in the ultra-modern Therme Vals.

GERMANY

travel essentials

TIME ZONE: GMT +1

TELEPHONE CODE: +49

CURRENCY: Euro

CAPITAL: Berlin

LANGUAGE: German

WHEN TO GO: Germany's climate is almost as varied as its culture, but extreme temperature highs and lows are rare. Summers average between 20° and 30°C (68° and 86°F), although frequent showers can be unpredictable. Winters are generally cold.

Bad Elster

This fine old spa town in Saxony sits sheltered by a dense natural barrier of wooded hills on the banks of the picturesque River Weiße Elster.

INFORMATION

ALBERTSBAD

t +49 374 375 3900 *(book through tourist office)*

Contains several therapy suites, sauna area, indoor pools and whirlpool baths. From €20 for a bath and massage package.

SÄCHSISCHEN STAATSBAD

t +49 374 377 1111

w www.saechsische-staatsbaeder.de

The Velvet and Silk one-day package, which includes a massage, Rasul and entrance to the baths and saunas, costs from €77.

ABOVE *Flower-filled spa gardens.*

OPPOSITE *Albertsbad – Bad Elster's fine public bathhouse.*

PREVIOUS PAGE *View of Baden-Baden (see page 45).*

Untouched by bombs or invasion, Bad Elster was once the favoured resort of the holidaying Russian Red Army, who descended on this charming mountain wellness sanctuary for a much-needed get-away-from-it-all. Together with Saxony's other state spa, Bad Brambach, this distinguished health resort has purveyed wellness for over 150 years. After the launch of the first official spa bathing season in 1848 by the royal family of Saxony, Bad Elster fast became renowned for its coarse, therapeutic mud and 11 sparkling medicinal springs. However, the healing properties of the local waters were recognized well before the 19th century. The physician to Duke Moritz von Sachsen-Zeitz first spotted their curative powers in 1669 when he noticed that those that took to the waters appeared to benefit from improved levels of health and vitality – with dramatic effect.

Public Bathhouse

A string of handsome colonnades and stylish buildings lead to Bad Elster's public bathhouse, the **Albertsbad**, built just before the outbreak of the First World War. Seemingly lost in time, the spa retains an imperial-style splendour with carved wood, splendid Meissen porcelain and a plush new reproduction swimming pool that has opulent columns, domes and spires. Set in idyllic scenery with peaceful gardens for relaxation, this mud-therapy centre is renowned for its wide range of health and wellness cures. Stimulating mineral and bubble baths are applied in copper tubs from the time of King Friedrich August II. Curative mud baths and hot sludgy mud packs are specialities here. Though the town's baths stagnated under communism, requiring both refurbishment and reinvigoration, they have since flourished to fully captilize on reunited Germany's wellness boom.

State Spa

Most first-time visitors to Bad Elster try a hotchpotch of traditional therapies to sample a wide range of natural health options at the **Sächsischen Staatsbad** (Saxon State Spa). Choose from bathing rituals that include waters containing carbon dioxide, minerals or dehydrated gases or decide on a slow, oily full-body massage or brave a drinking cure. Spacious pools and sauna areas are set at different temperatures and are equipped with massage nozzles, whirlpools and a variety of steam features. After successive gently fizzing dips and baths, treat your body to a herbal body emulsion and aromatic massage – the treatments on offer run from traditional, firm German-style rubs using beer and floral petals to sensual hot-stone massages. Exercise is offered in the surrounding parklands among fountains and well-tended herbaceous borders.

3 things you must not miss

1 Alte Schloss

Visit the remains of the Alte Schloss (Old Castle), which date back to the 12th century. They are situated 2km (1¼ miles) north-west of Bad Elster's centre. *www.bad-elster.de*

2 Hike to the Border

Hike across 10km (6¼ miles) of leafy country trails to the Czech border through the region's resplendent Naturpark Erzgebirge/Vogtland, crossing woodlands, grasslands and emerald valleys. *www.natur park-erzgebirge-vogtland.de*

▶ 3 NaturTheater

Stroll around the gorgeous NaturTheater in its picturesque, natural woodland setting. This is the oldest open-air theatre in Saxony and is home to a six-month season of opera, concerts and cinema. *www.naturtheater-badelster.de*

Wiesbaden

The gateway to the lush, green Rheingau region, the spa town of Wiesbaden has an illustrious history and is one of Germany's fine old-style health resorts.

ABOVE Open-air bathing at the Opelbad.

OPPOSITE Kaiser-Friedrich-Therme: handsome art nouveau grandeur.

With 26 hot, steam-shrouded springs and a bygone architectural elegance synonymous with the glorious Wilhelmina era, the city is peppered with green, plant-filled gardens and is renowned for its year-round calendar of cultural events that take place on the banks of the Rhine. Hailed for its curative properties since Roman times, Wiesbaden has been inextricably linked with wellness and healing for centuries. Over the years, the beneficial qualities of the mineral-packed waters have been utilized in a variety of therapeutic ways, from summer bathing in outdoor pools to medicinal dips and underwater massage in the thermal suites of stylish, purpose-built spa centres.

Spa Experience

Today, Wiesbaden's most notable buildings include the art nouveau-style **Kaiser-Friedrich-Therme** and the ultra-modern **Thermalbad Aukammtal**. Both are celebrated wellness temples that offer a wide array of sauna and spa packages to soothe mind, body and soul.

Built on the site of an old Roman sauna, the Kaiser-Friedrich-Therme evokes the charm of Emperor Wilhelm's reign. Careful and extensive restoration, reconstruction and remodelling in 1999 has ensured the long-term survival of this fine building and it has retained many of its fine embellishments, valuable ceramics and frescoes thanks to the painstaking project that conserved its grand, period style.

In contrast, the modern Thermalbad Aukammtal has six state-of-the-art saunas together with an indoor and outdoor thermal bathing pool, where mixed- and single-sex social dips and drenching sessions run for 362 days of the year.

Pleasant Surroundings

While the city continues to uphold a sterling reputation for the easing of rheumatic and orthopaedic ailments, the healing waters of

3 things you **must not** miss

◀ 1 Schloss Biebrich
Enjoy a day out at the opulent Schloss Biebrich (Biebrich Palace). It's extensive riverside grounds are wonderful to wander around. *www.wiesbaden.de*

2 City's Tallest Building
Visit the mid-19th century neo-Gothic, triple-naved Marktkirche (Market Church). With its 92-m (302-ft) west tower, it is the city's tallest building. *www.wiesbaden.de*

3 Picnic Spot
Climb up Neroberg Hill for stunning, jaw-dropping views across the whole of Wiesbaden. This is the perfect peaceful picnic spot.

At less than €20 for a 4-hour session, the basic thermal package at this fine, historical spa venue is good value. You can add in pampering: classic German massage (40–90 minutes) for €40–100 or choose from a range of body wraps, €50–120.

This thermal bathing complex is modern, high-tech and family friendly (children aged 2+). Bathing is €8.50, sauna suite €15 and full-body massages from €50 (some using honey and herbs).

This scenic bathing venue is extremely popular in summer (open May–September). Entry from €7.

Wiesbaden are also just as famous today for the fun and relaxation they offer during the sun-soaked summer months. Ranking high among the most scenic bathing venues is the **Opelbad**. Located on Wiesbaden's picturesque Neroberg Hill, it offers spellbinding views across the city from a beautiful pool fed by hot springs. A variety of sauna, pampering programmes and different massage therapies are also available.

Visitors can orientate themselves using Wiesbaden's Kurhaus (Spa House), the city's iconic focal point and main landmark. Built in 1907 under the aegis of Kaiser Wilhelm II, these imposing structures are surrounded by English-style flower-filled gardens and are instantly recognizable for their fine portico of giant columns and adjacent spa colonnade (constructed in 1827), the longest columned hall in Europe. Enjoy a stroll in the landscaped grounds at the rear of the spa buildings through gardens dotted with magnolias, azaleas, rhododendrons and cypress trees to marvel at fountains, ponds, statues and sculpture together with Wiesbaden's highly ornate, shell-shaped bandstand.

The city is also renowned for its handsome old quarter, where narrow, winding streets lined with houses built in the 18th and 19th centuries converge at the Bäckerbrunnen fountain on Grabenstraße – a popular meeting place. However, it is the area closest to the old Roman gate that draws the most tourists thanks to the 15 different springs that flow into the Kochbrunnen drinking fountain. This was once Wiesbaden's hotspot for ingesting cups of curative waters.

RIGHT The Kurhaus is the town's most famous landmark.

Baden-Baden

Of the many dozens of traditional spa towns that are home to Germany's 900-plus wellness resorts, Baden-Baden (meaning Bathing-Bathing) is the most famous.

ABOVE *Trinkhalle, Baden-Baden's pump room.*

In Germany's southern reaches, the wellness appeal of the region stems from a wholesome climate and age-old thermal springs. Baden-Baden forms the heart of Germany's spa heritage and is where the Romans first appreciated the hot mineral springs, founding the town and naming it 'Aquae' (Waters) in honour of its healing powers. You can visit the 2,000-year-old Roman bath ruins, the Römische Badruinen, which are some of the country's oldest and best-kept examples. The ruins are located underneath the Römerplatz. The museum entrance is via the Steinstraße or the Friedrichsbad underground car park.

Visiting European aristocracy arrived in the 18th and 19th centuries, frequenting the baths fed by 24 springs that pump out almost 1,000,000 litres (220,000 gallons) every day from 1.5-km (1-mile) deep subterranean primeval reservoirs.

Traditional Bathing

Set within a deep, lush basin, balmy Baden-Baden is sheltered from the harsh German winter, offering elegant sanctuary in its ancient, steam-cloaked bathhouses to those keen to strip off, chill out and relax. As in most of Germany's wellness resorts, bare flesh and good health go hand in hand and Baden-Baden's casual approach to clothing is suitably continental. In the 125-year-old all-nude **Friedrichsbad** clothing isn't optional, it is surplus to requirements, allowing the health-giving springs to work their magic directly on stressed-out, fatigued limbs. Marvel at elaborate frescoes around a highly decorated awe-inspiring central dome and breathe in the aromas that provide a sensory treat for body and soul.

Amid marble, brass columns and decorative tiles, this graceful experience in the Römisch-Irisches Bad (Roman-Irish

3 things you **must not** miss

1 Casino
Join the high rollers at Baden-Baden's neon-lit casino. At 200 years old, it is the oldest casino in Germany and is decorated in the style of a historic French château. *www.casino-baden-baden.de*

2 Museum Frieder Burda
One of Germany's most extensive collections of modern art. Houses some stunning post-war expressionist paintings as part of an exhibit of 580 works; mainly German but also includes some works by fine international artists. *www.sammlung-frieder-burda.de*

▶ 3 A Day at the Races
At the Iffezheim racetrack thoroughbred steeds and noble riders uphold a tradition dating back to 1858. The track, near Baden-Baden, nestles between the Rhine and the Black Forest – a most romantic setting. *www.baden-racing.com*

FRIEDRICHSBAD

t +49 7221 2759 20
w www.carasana.de

The experience at this historic spa centres on a 16-step cleansing ritual. A single-admission ticket, including soap and brush massage (8 minutes), 3½ hours, is €31.

AQUASANA, VILLA QUISISANA-SUITE HOTEL AND SPA

t +49 7221 3690
w www.quisisana-baden-baden.de

Revel in the relaxing peace of the AquaSana sauna and bathing wellness complex where bubbling, steaming and massaging waters flow as part of a comprehensive wellness programme. Book the bath with meadow flowers for a splurge (€30).

DORINT MAISON MESSMER

t +49 7221 30120
w www.dorint.com

For unabashed luxury book this five-star gem. A Relaxing Day, which includes a full-body peel, a soft-pack body wrap and an aromatic pamper massage is €175.

ABOVE The Kurhaus (Spa Rooms) is home to one of the most famous casinos in Europe.

OPPOSITE Sumptuous bathing at the historic Friedrichsbad.

Bath) evokes the nostalgia of Roman bathing with health rituals that begin with a steamy, hot, invigorating shower followed by a warm-air bath. In vaulted tiled chambers a brisk rubdown with a soapsuds brush deeply cleanses the skin until it is so pink it almost squeaks. After yet another shower an ultra-misty stage of hot, steaming thermal baths follows before a final, cooler shower denotes that it is time for a dip in the restorative hot-spring baths. In a sulphur-rich shroud, each of the brackish pools varies dramatically in temperature and the sequence in which bathing occurs is an important part of the process. Men and women bathe separately or together, depending on the day of the week (see website), moving from one fog-cloaked cauldron to another in order to maximize the water's healing powers. It soothes and washes aches and pains away (together with any of the awkward

embarrassment of being nude) as several stages of bathing lead to the final pool, where you can experience the pounding beat of gushing cascades.

Modern Options

Bubbling waterfalls form the centrepiece of the nearby **AquaSana** wellness complex at the Villa Quisisana-Suite Hotel and Spa, where a sauna and bathing suite contains thermal pools, steam rooms, Turkish baths and a variety of showers and tubs.

Epitomizing Baden-Baden's charming old-world elegance, the upscale **Dorint Maison Messmer** hotel mixes historic quaintness with modern-day therapeutic rewards. In-room pleasure tubs are a feature of the hotel or visit the on-site spa centre for steam baths, whirlpools and age-old water-based health rituals, which will help to ease tensions and relax the mind.

Allgäu

A deep-rooted wellness tradition prevails amid a stunning landscape that offers soft hills and alpine meadows, steep slopes and summits, and emerald forests and rocky crystal-clear streams.

ABOVE Allgäu's meadows are full of flowers in spring.

OPPOSITE Spa resort of Bad Hindelang.

Over 50 spas are located in forested Bavaria – Germany's self-proclaimed 'Region of Vitality' – with around a dozen found in Allgäu. Wellness tourism dates back over 100 years in the region between the River Iller in the west and the Lech in the east, the Allgäu Alps in the south and the Ries basin. Rest, relaxation and recreation centre on walks and hikes along well-marked trails, trekking from hut to hut. Famous local priest Father Sebastian Kneipp laid the foundation for his ground-breaking health philosophies in this area. The Bad Wörishofen medical guru advocated water cures, a balanced diet and physical exercise – a philosophy that continues to be followed to this day.

Modern Allgäu is home to numerous award-winning wellness resorts and spas, Alpine hotels and thermal springs in an idyllic countryside location close to the state border with neighbouring Baden-Württemberg (where there are also over 60 highly regarded spa hotels and health resorts built around innumerable mineral springs). Wellness had been a standard concept in the Allgäu region long before it became a recognized fashion, with therapy menus centred on the blessings bestowed on the region by Mother Nature.

Mother Nature's Pampering

Germany's only Alpine allergy station is on Mount Oberjoch in the spa resort municipality of Bad Hindelang, where the locals claim the air is purer than anywhere else in the country. A popular destination with allergy sufferers and their families, who find the clear air free from dust mites, mould fungus spores, pollen and pollution, the wellness ethos of the six towns that make up the Bad Hindelang spa resort centres on a holistic health concept. Five climate spas and plenty of small hotels have already been awarded the 'Premium-Class' accolade for their innovative products and services.

3 things you **must not** miss

◄ 1 Fairytale Palace
Visit the opulent Schloss Linderhof, one of the most alluring, fairytale-like buildings in Germany, with its beautiful parklands studded with fountains. *www.schloss linderhof.de*

2 Winter Sports
Head to the Allgäu Alps in winter for a wide range of ski areas of all sizes for downhill skiers, snowboarders and cross-country skiers of all skill standards. *www.bayerisch-schwaben.info*

3 Art and Architecture
Art and architectural buffs will find plenty of interest within the walls, museums and galleries of the medieval towns of Dillingen, Donauwörth, Kaufbeuren, Memmingen, Mindelheim and Nördlingen. *www.bayern.by/de*

A half-dozen wellness centres also offer a wide range of health, well-being and beautification rituals, such as those offered by the **Hotel Bären**. This hotel is engulfed by the scenic splendour of the Allgäu Alps, where country-style rooms with modern amenities and an attractive range of wellness services are offered, together with nutritional hearty regional cuisine. Relax in the indoor pool, sauna and steam bath, or chill out on a sun-facing terrace before making full use of a therapeutic treatment menu that features a de luxe herbal massage with leisurely, slow, synchronized strokes that is delightfully unhurried.

As the second-largest village in Bad Hindelang, Bad Oberdorf is home to Germany's highest sulphur spring. This is a quaint health resort with a well-preserved traditional Allgäu ambience that has been used since the 19th century. Here, the earth-tone sauna suites and therapy rooms at the **Alpenlandhotel Hirsch** entice wellness tourists into a blissful state of relaxation using whirlpool mineral baths, hot tubs, steam and sensual massage.

HOTEL BÄREN

t +49 8324 9304 0
w www.baeren-
     hindelang.de

*A sumptuous 1-hour
massage using local curative
herbs is €65.*

ALPENLANDHOTEL
HIRSCH

t + 49 8324 308
w www.alpenlandhotel.de

*Enjoy high-quality sauna,
shower, steam and whirlpool
treatments in a purpose-built
aqua-therapy treatment
suite, from €45.*

HUBERTUS – ALPIN
LODGE & SPA

t +49 8328 9200
w www.hotel-hubertus.de

*Opt for a delectable Alpine
massage with soft, rich oils
infused with meadow
flowers, priced at €98 for
60 unforgettable minutes.*

KNEIPP-KURHOTEL UND
WELLNESSHOTEL
FÖRCH

t +49 8247 3960
w www.kurhotel-foerch.de

*Therapies centre on
endemic herbs and flowers
and local healing waters.
Expect to pay €50 for a
tension-busting jet-water
massage.*

ABOVE *Alpine splendour at
the Hubertus – Alpin Lodge
& Spa.*

Another highlight, this time in the municipality of Balderschwang, is the **Hubertus – Alpin Lodge & Spa**, where the treatments involve using locally grown ingredients such as wild berries, Alpine plants and edelweiss. As fresh mountain breezes waft the sweet fragrances of nature into the spa environs, a vast array of natural wellness treatments vie for your attention. Choose from four-night deals or opt for à la carte therapies, such as algae body wraps with mallow extract, silky Alpine body packs and mountain-spring baths.

Hay, Herbs and Alpine Flowers

The ready availability of authentic hydrotherapy as Kneipp conceived it is perhaps the greatest revelation for first-timers in Allgäu and it is a speciality of the spas in the retreat of Bad Wörishofen. This town has bracing mountain air, flower gardens, cobbled streets and a pretty river and, as the home of Kneipp, it extols the virtue of a restful sleep 'nature's way'. To do it in traditional style, sleep overnight in a warm hay sack infused with 21 different kinds of herbs and flowers. On waking, guests are treated to the 'interaction of the earth's five elements' in treatments that combine hydrotherapy, exercise therapy, phytotherapy, nutrition and a balanced lifestyle. Expect to be nicely pummelled by a series of water-jet massages, before arm baths and half an hour of vigorous leg wading prior to a healthy lunch.

Wellness therapies to treat cardiovascular disorders, neurovegetative illnesses, digestive complaints and metabolic problems utilize the ethos of Kneipp's legacy. Throughout the town is a variety of relaxing, healing bathing venues, pools, saunas, steam rooms and whirlpools.

Each Kneipp therapy at the much-acclaimed **Kneipp-Kurhotel und Wellnesshotel Förch** is highly recommended. Here a trusted menu of traditional treatments has been given an irresistible modern twist to fuse health-giving Asian touch therapies with German botanicals and traditional healing know-how.

AUSTRIA

travel essentials

TIME ZONE: GMT +1

TELEPHONE CODE: +43

CURRENCY: Euro

CAPITAL: Vienna

LANGUAGE: German

WHEN TO GO: Mountain resorts have a winter sports calendar and a season for summer hikers. In between times, many tourist facilities are closed. Urban centres are popular year-round, with tourist numbers swelling during peak holidays and annual festivals. Visit during May to August for the best of the warm weather, while snow is pretty much guaranteed November until early April.

Vienna

Creamy, velvety, rich chocolate is used as a curative, wellness therapy in Austria's refined capital city where decadent, cocoa-laden, nourishing treatments are delightfully calorie-free.

ABOVE Cocoa beans are full of flavonoids.

OPPOSITE Gardens of the Schönbrunn Palace, one of the most popular sightseeing destinations in Vienna.

PREVIOUS PAGE Rogner Bad Blumau, Styria (see page 55).

Austrian chocolate took Vienna by storm in the middle of the 19th century as sweet-makers clamoured to create Europe's richest, creamiest confectionery. It was Austrian confectioners who transformed a frothy, bitter drink into handmade solid chocolate much beloved by the gourmand-loving aristocratic classes, fuelling an Austrian passion for blended cream, caramel, cocoa, sugar and rich cocoa butter that survives to this day. None of these talented chocolate-making pioneers could have foreseen the role chocolate would play in society a century or so later – especially in Austria's fine, historic capital city.

Sacher Spa

Chocolate tantalizes our taste buds to an ecstatic high as we revel in its sensual delights. Yet it is not just ingestion that offers physical- and mood-enhancing qualities, according to therapists at Vienna's much-reputed **Sacher Spa** at the Hotel Sacher. Chocolate eases pain as joy, pleasure and elation are experienced, provoking a mix of chemical dependency and unbridled decadent want that prompts a stratospheric hike in feel-good factor every time we take a bite. At the Sacher Spa, therapies exploit our natural dermal rate of absorption to allow these feelings of euphoria to be transported to our brains during chocolate-laden nourishing treatments. Cocoa has higher antioxidant potential than green tea or red wine and contains health-giving mineral salts and vitamins. In non-ingested forms, our bodies can benefit from huge amounts of sweet-smelling chocolate as it can stimulate positive energy while satisfying sweet-toothed desire – without a single calorie being consumed.

The Sacher Spa is housed in a landmark Viennese building where the unique chocolate cake, the original Sacher-torte,

3 things you **must not** miss

◀ 1 Composers' Homes
Acclaimed maestros Beethoven, Mozart, Strauss and Schubert have all called Vienna home; music lovers should be sure to see at least one of their former houses. *www.wien.info*

2 River Cruise
Journey the languid waters of the mighty River Danube on a morning, afternoon or twilight cruise along Europe's most fabled waterway. *www.wien.info*

3 Domkirche St Stephan
Stroll through the Innere Stadt's historic quarter to marvel at the ornate Gothic splendour of St Stephen's Cathedral and its bustling plaza. *www.stephanskirche.at*

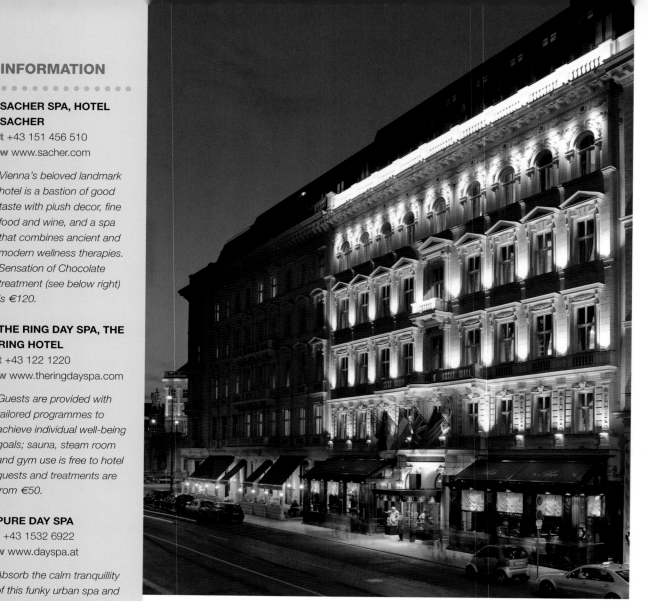

ABOVE *The Hotel Sacher.*

SACHER SPA, HOTEL SACHER

t +43 151 456 510
w www.sacher.com

Vienna's beloved landmark hotel is a bastion of good taste with plush decor, fine food and wine, and a spa that combines ancient and modern wellness therapies. Sensation of Chocolate treatment (see below right) is €120.

THE RING DAY SPA, THE RING HOTEL

t +43 122 1220
w www.theringdayspa.com

Guests are provided with tailored programmes to achieve individual well-being goals; sauna, steam room and gym use is free to hotel guests and treatments are from €50.

PURE DAY SPA

t +43 1532 6922
w www.dayspa.at

Absorb the calm tranquillity of this funky urban spa and enjoy the high-quality therapies, such as a nourishing 55-minute hand massage (€50).

was created by Franz Sacher in 1832. Today, the Hotel Sacher – established by Eduard Sacher, son of the Sacher-torte's creator – pays homage to the family's sweet-toothed heritage with a range of chocolate-laden lotions, potions, scrubs and wraps at the Sacher Spa. Choose from an array of cocoa-enriched masks, sensuous face creams and rich, milky chocolate moisturizers – all of them can be used guilt-free. During the 60-minute Sensation of Chocolate therapy, a feeling of wellness envelops you as serotonin levels and feel-good endorphins are treated to a serious boost. Revel in milk, white and dark chocolate aromas as a healing brownie mix warms against the skin amid visions of whipped cream with frostings. You'll leave feeling divine and smelling good enough to eat – without adding an inch to your waistline.

Other notable spas in the city include **The Ring Day Spa** at The Ring Hotel, and **Pure Day Spa** where chocolate therapies are an occasional feature.

Styria

This region, located to the south of the city of Graz, is dubbed 'Austria's Natural Spa Capital'. It is home to a rich curative tradition and is known as Thermenland Styria.

Set among gently rolling hills, tufts of vines, pumpkin fields, orchards and castles, Thermenland is famous for its attractive spa towns, including Bad Waltersdorf, Bad Blumau and Loipersdorf. These are three of the six settlements in the region blessed with hot-water springs. Rising up from a depth of around 3,000m (9,843ft), the mineral-packed waters have long been the basis of the well-being therapies on offer in the region.

With spectacular scenery, a wealth of countryside activities, numerous bathing options, therapeutic treatment centres, beauty salons and relaxation areas, Thermenland Styria offers an all-round package for wellness tourists.

Bad Waltersdorf

Styria's popular Bad Waltersdorf spa resort takes great pride in its thermal waters and is renowned for its first-class well-being facilities. At the town's **Heiltherme** thermal spa, waters are pumped in at 36°C (97°F) year-round to fill seven bathing pools in a 4,000-sq m (43,000-sq ft) thermal complex. There is also a Roman sauna shower area, sauna village with a dozen cabins, ice room and wellness park, where a wide variety of health and fitness programmes are offered. If you want some exercise, bird-filled country paths allow plenty of opportunity to explore Bad Waltersdorf on foot or by bike.

Bad Blumau

In peaceful Bad Blumau even the most discerning spa-goers will relish the funky, high-concept, stylish ambience of the **Rogner Bad Blumau**. A string of bizarre colourful facades, curves and domes dominate the building, with a ring-shaped spa at the centre and swimming, bathing and restaurant areas that reach out like tentacles into open, grassy meadows. Pools are fed

ABOVE Hot-water bathing pools at the Heiltherme.

3 things you **must not** miss

1 Take a Hike
Explore the rugged hiking trails of the north-west Styria region of Schladming-Dachstein extending from the Dachstein Massif to the Grimming. *www.schladming-dachstein.at*

2 Sample Local Wine
Visit any Styrian village to experience the rustic charm of a *buschenschank* (rural cafe): a local tasting room for the region's excellent Sauvignon Blanc. *www.buschenschank.at*

▶ **3 Castle Ruins**
A stroll up to and around the magnificent Burgruine Gösting (Gösting Castle Ruins) offers spectacular views across the city of Graz. *www.graztourismus.at*

from the local natural hot spring, with the resort's famous Vulkania hot spring (complete with fake glowing red volcano!) a kooky homage to Bad Blumau's healing heritage.

Loipersdorf

Similarly upscale, although along much more conventional lines, the spa resort of Loipersdorf is home to the purpose-built bathing and sauna complex of **Schaffelbad**.

Tucked among vineyards and horse-riding trails, the complex was designed as a necklace of relaxation pools in the form of lakes, lagoons, basins, streams and whirlpools. The resort is distinctive for its clothes-optional bathing and rest areas, together with its 14 high-tech aromatic and infra-red sauna zones – an unforgettable wellness treat, especially when combined with a fragrant Styria wine bath.

RIGHT Rogner Bad Blumau – stylish, chic and relaxing.

CZECH REPUBLIC

travel essentials

TIME ZONE: GMT +1

TELEPHONE CODE: +420

CURRENCY: Czech crown

CAPITAL: Prague

LANGUAGE: Czech

WHEN TO GO: The Czech Republic is situated in a temperate zone and boasts four distinct seasons of equal length. Winters are relatively mild (at around -2°C/28°F) and summers rarely exceed 22°C (72°F).

Karlovy Vary

In the UNESCO-status historic Spa Triangle, the balneological resources of Karlovy Vary are fully utilized by a fine collection of elegant spa buildings in a scenic location along a picturesque river.

ABOVE Aquatherapy at the Parkhotel Richmond.

OPPOSITE Karlovy Vary – a town with a lengthy wellness tradition.

PREVIOUS PAGE Mariánské Lázně (see page 63).

With its numerous thermal springs, the town has a lengthy history as a wellness resort, attracting the great and the good with its curative waters since the Middle Ages. It is home to the hottest mineral springs in the Czech Republic – the Vřídlo – a steamy, bubbling jet that rises to the earth's surface at a temperature of 73.4°C (164°F), spurting forth at a velocity of 2,000 litres (440 gallons) per minute, gushing 14m (46ft) into the air.

Picture-perfect Town

Named after Emperor Charles (Karel) IV, the historic centre of Karlovy Vary (also known in English as Carlsbad) is ringed by wooded slopes in a deep valley of the Teplá River. Dotted with lookout towers and summer houses, Karlovy Vary is looped by a tentacle of bird-filled walking trails that weave through pretty forest parks on the outer fringes of town. Marvellous frothy stucco-rich buildings in delicate pastel hues give the town the mouth-watering appeal of giant fondant-filled patisserie. A simple Karlovy Vary pleasure is to sit among the historical buildings in the main colonnade and admire the curvaceous cast iron, polished woods and bold, stained glass in the most stunning designs.

Natural Aquatherapy

Highlights in Karlovy Vary include the grand old-world spa at the **Parkhotel Richmond**, housed in a truly resplendent mansion set among mature trees and expansive grounds on the banks of the Teplá River. Specializing in anti-stress, anti-ageing, slimming, detoxification, relaxation and general wellness programmes, the Richmond offers a range of menus from full weekends to seven-night stays. Using the legacies of Karlovy Vary's lengthy healing tradition, most programmes centre on aquatherapy, underwater massage, carbonic baths and drinking cures together with nutritional advice.

3 things you **must not** miss

◀ 1 Majestic Church

Take a gentle walk up to the Kostel sv. Máří Magdaleny (Church of St Mary Magdalene), which dates back to 1736. It is perched on top of a hill overlooking the Vřídlo spring. *www.karlovy-vary.cz/en/cirkevni-stavby*

2 Local Speciality

Try the famous sweet delicacy known as 'Carlsbad plums'. The plums are candied in hot syrup, then halved and stuffed into dried damsons.

3 Film Festival

The town's highly regarded international film festival is held annually in the first week of July. The films are shown in a number of Karlovy Vary's historic venues. *www.kviff.com*

● ● ● ● ● ● ● ● ● ● ● ● ● ●

PARKHOTEL RICHMOND

t +420 353 177 111
w www.richmond.cz

Visitors rave about the seven-day anti-ageing programme, priced from just €470, including accommodation, meals, 21 treatments and use of the pools and sauna.

SPA HOTEL BRISTOL

t + 420 353 344 444
w www.bristol.cz

One night full board with a spa treatment is €109. Special rates and seasonal discounts are available for longer stays.

ABOVE *Spa gardens and nature trails at the Parkhotel Richmond.*

RIGHT *Thermal geysers spurt hot waters at Vřídlo spring.*

Another notable favourite is the **Spa Hotel Bristol**, a collection of fine old buildings that make up a wellness complex, offering a variety of accommodation from standard to ultra-de luxe. Almost every therapy on the Bristol's comprehensive spa menu utilizes the saline-rich thermal waters drawn from a depth of around 2,000m (6,561ft). Besides age-old drinking cures there is a range of classic hydrotherapeutic procedures and baths that aid in the treatment of metabolic disorders, digestive ailments and weight loss, among other conditions. Programmes at the Bristol also promote the importance of experiencing the natural environment, with hikes and walks in the spa's woods an integral part of daily wellness therapies. A trio of walking trails lead from the building's main entrance, each passes through spectacular valley scenery and takes about 50 minutes to complete.

Františkovy Lázně

Set among trees and gardens where grand pavilions have been built over numerous bubbling springs, the town is home to some particularly well-preserved spa heritage buildings.

Although officially founded in 1793 and named after Emperor Franz (František) III, the healing springs had already gained prominence for their curative strength in the Middle Ages. Although built for the most part in the period of classicism, like neighbouring Mariánské Lázně (see page 63), Františkovy Lázně is very different in layout and character. It was built to an orthogonal plan, with densely lined streets of classicist, Empire and historicist buildings and is scattered with imposing sculptures.

All three of West Bohemia's spa towns have attracted countless rulers, politicians, writers, composers and celebrities to their wellness springs, from such historical figures as Russian tsar Peter the Great to members of the Rockefeller and Rothschild families and countless models and TV stars. Numerous myths and legends surround the Spa Triangle. For example, in Františkovy Lázně, every woman trying to conceive still visits the statue of Little Franz in the town's

park. According to legend, just one touch of the statue will ensure conception so that she'll give birth to a baby within a year.

Baths, Wraps and Showers

At the family-run **Hotel Francis**, less than five minutes' walk from the main spa colonnade, the owners and their team pride themselves on their local knowledge. The hotel can arrange all manner of natural curative therapies that draw on Františkovy Lázně's spring waters, geothermal gases and sulphate-ferrous mud.

The ultra-swish **Francis Palace** offers a fine array of therapies on site, drawing water up from the town's own springs. Choose from around 50 different spa treatments – from carbonic baths, mineral showers and peat wraps to decadent, leisurely oil-rich massages using gently applied strokes to specific meridian points to help release blockages and restore and balance the flow of energy throughout the body.

ABOVE Glauber Springs Hall.

3 things you **must not** miss

1 Volcanic Activities
Enjoy a day trip out to Komorní Hůrka, the youngest volcano in Central Europe, set within a lush, green conservation zone amid staggering natural beauty. *http://cestovani.kr-karlovarsky.cz*

2 Historic Church
Marvel at the fine Kostel Povýšení sv. Kříže (Church of the Assumption of the Holy Cross) built in 1815–19. It is located in Jiraskova Street, facing the Glauber Springs Hall right in the heart of town.

▶ 3 Slavkov Forest
Journey out to this picturesque, protected forest, where flower-filled woodlands and important areas of vast raised bog form part of a huge natural water reservoir that is home to numerous bird species. *www.marianskelazne.cz*

INFORMATION

HOTEL FRANCIS
t +420 354 541 049
w www.hotelfrancis.cz

*Located less than a
2-minute walk from the spa
park, this well-run family-
owned hotel offers top-
notch service and organizes
therapies for guests, from
spa days to à la carte
treatments. Their Weekend
Wellness Stay, which
includes three treatments,
is CZK 2,990.*

FRANCIS PALACE
t +420 354 479 700
w www.francispalace.cz

*An aromatic massage at this
fine spa hotel is CZK 400.*

*RIGHT Glauber Springs pump
house gardens.*

Mariánské Lázně

Although less famous than its more high-profile neighbour Karlovy Vary, Mariánské Lázně's traditional curative history is equally impressive, stretching back well over 200 years.

Notable for its fine, cake-like spa buildings centred on a leafy, landscaped park established in the 19th century, Mariánské Lázně is characterized by a 200-year wellness tradition that blends ancient health principles with modern therapeutic procedures. Visitors can enjoy over 100 spa therapies in a spa area that exceeds 20,000sq m (215,276sq ft), where use of local natural therapeutic resources focuses on mineral springs, peat, the naturally occurring 'Maria's gas' and the healing power of touch. Distinctive for its charming gazebos, garden houses and handsome colonnades, Mariánské Lázně's wooded valley widens to form the heart of the town where verdant slopes extend downstream.

Well-being Wonderland

Overlooking handsome villas and grand examples of art nouveau architecture, the majestic **Danubius Health Spa Resort**

Nové Lázně enjoys a privileged location nestled into a verdant slope in the centre of the spa park close to the town's impressive colonnades. One of the most historically rich buildings in the Czech Republic, the hotel has marble columns dating back to 1896, together with a host of neo-Renaissance architectural touches in a classic structure built in 1827. Designed as luxurious accommodation for notable guests, the original building work was funded by the Teplá Monastery. In years gone by, guests would bathe in the on-site Roman spa and royal cabin's bubble bath once used by King Edward VII. Today, the Nové Lázně is renowned for its extensive hydrotherapy menu of mineral bathing, wet packs, massages, inhalation and colonic irrigation together with dry CO_2 gas baths.

The 157-room **Danubius Health Spa Resort Centrální Lázně** is the oldest of the town's treasure trove of spa buildings.

3 things you **must not** miss

1 Town Museum
Browse a captivating collection of ancient relics of cultural and historical importance to the town at the Městské muzeum Mariánské Lázně (Town Museum), housed in a fine old mansion house built in 1818. *www.marianskelazne. cz/en/kultura/town-museum/*

2 Winter Sport
Experience an unforgettable winter on the town's super-fast, sleek, snow-cloaked slopes, which hosted the World Ski Championships in 2007. *www.marianskelazne. cz/en/sport/ski-complex-of-marianske-lazne/*

▶ 3 Historic Sites
Marvel at the ancient castles of Bečov and Loket, tucked in the picturesque surrounding countryside or the fine chateau of Kynžvart and grand Teplá Monastery, with its well-planned herbal, flower and vegetable gardens. *www.czechtourism.com*

INFORMATION

DANUBIUS HEALTH SPA RESORT NOVÉ LÁZNĚ

t +420 354 644 111
w www.danubiushotels.com

Tucked into hillside woodlands and greenery in the centre of the spa park, this elegant spa hotel epitomizes Mariánské Lázně's bygone splendour and offers to-die-for herb oil massages from €65.

DANUBIUS HEALTH SPA RESORT CENTRÁLNÍ LÁZNĚ

t +420 354 634 111
w www.danubiushotels.com

As the town's most traditional spa building set on the source of Maria's Spring, this fine hotel has the largest and most authentic spa, with 54 treatment cabins and an array of old-meets-new therapies, from €70.

A handsome complex built in grand style, it benefits from the rising surge of Maria's Spring directly beneath. With a composition of nearly 100 per cent natural carbon dioxide, therapies centre on curative steam and gas together with organic peat wraps. A Roman-style bathing venue has a trio of pools, whirlpools and a sauna, as well as plenty of relaxation space. Choose from a variety of massage therapies on a large wellness menu, including hot stone, aromatherapy and forest herbs. Cooling showers also make the most of Mariánské Lázně's naturally surging ferrite acidulous waters, which spout forth at less than 10°C (50°F) from 40 underground wells.

ABOVE *Spa colonnade.*

RIGHT *Bathing house at Danubius Health Spa Resort Nové Lázně.*

OPPOSITE *Early 19th-century pseudo-baroque cast-iron spa colonnade.*

SLOVAKIA

travel essentials

TIME ZONE: GMT +1

TELEPHONE CODE: +421

CURRENCY: Euro

CAPITAL: Bratislava

LANGUAGE: Slovak

WHEN TO GO: Bloom-filled April and May brings zest and vigour to Slovakia after what are typically cold, dark, cloudy winters. Bright, cool and breezy summers are ideal for outdoor pursuits, with sunshine that runs well into September and October.

Piešt'any

Derived from the Latin word *paskan* (meaning 'sand'), this is Slovakia's most famous spa town. It was named by early settlers, who built their settlements on sandy river deposits.

As Slovakia's longest watercourse, the Váh is a tributary of the mighty Danube, stretching for over 400km (248½ miles) along the country's northern and western flank. Prior to the arrival of Slovak tribes, during the Ice Age the unfrozen stretch of the river near some hot springs was used by animals as a watering place – a rare source of nourishment. Primeval hunters began to associate Piešt'any's alluring setting with enticing warmth – a quality that became all the more intriguing when a lame peacock with iridescent blue-green plumage was discovered near death on the riverbank. Dragging itself towards the spring-fed waters, the exhausted bird was badly injured and limp. Stunned by its beauty, the villagers gently lowered the bird into the Váh River. The peacock was miraculously cured, fanning its wings to display its tail feathers in all their shimmering glory to the wonderment of the crowd. Today, as a sacred bird of Greek goddess Hera, the peacock symbolizes Piešt'any's curative claims of eternal youth and embodies healing and restoration.

People from all over the world enjoy the wonderful natural healing riches of the spa town, with its highly acclaimed thermal springs (with temperatures as high as 70°C (158°F)) that are famous for their ability to soothe aches and pains. Among huge organic reserves of curative sulphur-bearing mud, Piešt'any has become inextricably linked with the 'magical' healing of all manner of rheumatic ills. Located in western Slovakia in Trnava County, this centre of age-old therapeutic waters and clay-rich soils offers numerous 'all-ills cures' focused on its gypsum-laden, milky-white pools.

Global Appeal

First settled in 1113, Piešt'any flourished during the early Middle Ages when a

ABOVE Small wooden church in the town.

OPPOSITE Piešt'any.

3 things you must not miss

1 Jazz nights
Enjoy lively music and the artisan scene at the friendly Art Jazz Gallery, where funky art and great jazz vibes combine in an impressive array of weekly gigs, events and showcases.
www.jazzpiestany.sk

2 Devil's Furnace
Stroll the archaeological cave site of Čertova pec (Devil's Furnace), 15km (9 miles) from Piešt'any's centre.
www.spapiestany.sk/en/trips-tours-and-coach-trips.html

▶ 3 Birdwatching
Take a summer boat ride along the Váh River and Lake Sĺňava for spectacular views across colourful flora to waterfowl on Bird Island.
www.spapiestany.sk/en/trips-tours-and-coach-trips.html

monastery first started organized bathing in the local waters. The monks preferred to attribute the curative success of the waters to the power of prayer. Later studies would reveal that the unique chemical composition of the water is conditioned by the geological stratification of the Považský Inovec Mountains. Formed from tiny clay-like particles swept into thermal wells, the town's gurgling bath-warm mud is packed with health-boosting natural bacteria while hot, steamy, thermal waters shrouded in a creamy haze are rich in organic sediment. As local practitioners became more adept at harnessing the powers of Mother Nature, Piešt'any's reputation for wellness spread and soon health pilgrims began to flock to the town in search of convalescence and good health.

By the end of the 18th century, spa buildings were being constructed around elaborate fountains and spouting springs of considerable international repute. The restorative qualities of the water attracted financiers, artists, athletes, politicians and doctors from all across Europe as well as Austro-Hungarian servicemen in need of recuperation during rare moments of leave. Bulgarian tsar Ferdinand I from the Coburg family was a frequent visitor to spas and during his stay in Piešt'any in 1917 he established his wartime staff there. German emperor Wilhelm II came for consultation and advice on the future leadership of the First World War and the last Austrian emperor Karol I also visited. Swedish writer and Nobel Prize winner for literature Selma Lagerlöf was a diehard Piešt'any faithful.

Austrian composer Johann Strauss Jun. and even Ludwig van Beethoven found inspiration in the peaceful leafy environs of the Váh River.

Today, Piešt'any has truly gone global, luring spa fans from as far afield as Asia, North America and Australia, with its transformational cocktail of over 60 traditional therapies. Arrive dead on your feet and jaded but leave bright-eyed, radiant and revived thanks to a hydro-therapeutic menu of mineral mudbaths, hot-mud body wraps, water-pressure massages, herbal foot baths, hot stones and nutrient-rich clay facials.

Warming Wellness Therapies

With Piešt'any's eternal-youth-giving peacock as its crest, the **Danubius Health Spa Resort Thermia Palace** enjoys resplendent views across the park-scattered Spa Island, the pretty garden-ringed curative oasis that forms the wellness epicentre of the town. Built in 1912, this fine art nouveau building sits directly on top of a subterranean thermal source. Marvel at a century-old balneotherapy centre designed by legendary spa architect Ármin Hegedüs that has required only partial renovation since its construction. Revel in the relaxing warmth and whimsical nostalgia amid old-time palatial elegance that combines dark wood panels, bold stained glass and peacock-inspired frescoes. Sense the history of the place, which in a bygone era was favoured by poets, sheikhs, maharajas, writers, kings and princesses.

The charming **Danubius Health Spa Resort Balnea Esplanade** is located among the foliage of Spa Island and offers a range of water therapies, such as fizzy carbon baths, underwater high-pressure jet massages and a wide range of multi-temperature hydrotherapy cures fed by springs containing 1,500mg of mineral substances per litre.

INFORMATION

DANUBIUS HEALTH SPA RESORT THERMIA PALACE
t +421 33 775 61 11
w www.danubiushotels.com

Indulge in a host of mineral-laden water therapies designed to soothe, ease tension, massage and deep cleanse. Special packages from €100 per night.

DANUBIUS HEALTH SPA RESORT BALNEA ESPLANADE
t +421 33 775 51 11
w www.danubiushotels.com

This 257-room wellness hotel is in a central location in the Spa Park and is connected to an impressive wellness centre, which offers guests a wide range of unique therapeutic and relaxation treatments. Discounted packages from €77 per night.

POLAND

travel essentials

TIME ZONE: GMT +1

TELEPHONE CODE: +48

CURRENCY: Złoty

CAPITAL: Warsaw

LANGUAGE: Polish

WHEN TO GO: Poland's weather is unpredictable with winters that vary dramatically in intensity from mild to bitterly cold. However, summers are generally warm and the most pleasant time to visit, with July the hottest month. September turns cool as October approaches, with colder weather increasing until December when the temperature drops below zero – sometimes to -20°C (-4°F).

Nałęczów

One of southern Poland's most established wellness resorts, this pretty town comprises paved garden-trimmed pathways scattered with benches, fountains, sculpture and plant-filled tubs.

Simply improving the general human condition is the goal of many fresh arrivals to the 19th-century garden town of Nałęczów. It is located 32km (20 miles) from the city of Lublin in the lush, green Nałęczów Plateau. The surrounding landscape has a geology rich in botanical resources such as mineral deposits, fertile lagoons, mud-filled wetlands, sparkling lakes, and fields and forests filled with healing plants, nuts, berries and blooms. Centred on a cardiology-focused 20ha (50-acre) spa park that is home to five clinics, sanatoriums and treatment suites, the town nestles in verdant low-lying terrain, 200m (656ft) above sea level where the mildly mineralized spring waters are traced with calcium bicarbonate and magnesium bicarbonate. (The thirst-quenching local libation – Naleczowianka – is Poland's most famous mineral water.) However, not every visitor to Nałęczów has a heart problem,

far from it. Hosts of yoga and massage-seeking wellness tourists and fresh-air freaks frequent the town too.

Surrounded by the hills of the Lublin Uplands, in the wooded valley of the River Bystra, Nałęczów has a pleasant springlike climate year-round. Centrally located, the town's extensive and beautifully manicured Park Zdrojowy (Spa Park), with its fully restored spa house and pretty ponds, is set among brightly coloured blooms, large mansion houses, leafy trees and broad avenues.

Trio of Wellness Hotels

Spa w Raju comprises of a trio of neighbouring wellness hotels owned by the same group, with each individual spa just 300m (984ft) from the others. Catering for different budgets and offering a full range of accommodation options – from luxury suites and apartments to basic rooms at

ABOVE Wood anemones grow wild in and around the town.

OPPOSITE Wawel Royal Castle, Kraków; just a short distance from Wieliczka (see page 75).

3 things you **must not** miss

1 Get Out of Town
Follow the town's riddle of walking trails to ravines and hills, villas immersed in impenetrable woods, green trees, birds and babbling brooks. www.naleczow.com.pl

2 Explore the Town
Stroll along the quaint villa-hemmed street of Armatnia Góra to the top of the hill past museums and galleries. Another peaceful walk along ulicę Lipowa passes by monuments and a baroque church. www.naleczow.com.pl

▶ **3 Historic Palace**
The town's most beloved historic monument, the Pałac Małachowskich (Malachowski's Palace), is a fine single-storey baroque-style building built in 1771–75 and surrounded by a park. www.naleczow.com.pl

SPA W RAJU

t +48 81 501 40 84
w www.spawraju.pl

A trio of spa hotels owned by the same group. Treatments can be booked across the three facilities with online discounts available. Their detoxifying oxygen microdermabrasion facial is priced at PLN 180 for face only, it is an additional PLN 120 for neck and décolleté.

WILLA MONIKA SPA

t +48 81 501 51 25
w www.willamonika.pl

Be prepared to be wowed by a vast menu of wellness therapy options, from soothing massages and restorative facials to a host of mud wraps, mineral scrubs and nourishing emulsions, from PLN 120.

HOTEL PRZEPIÓRECZKA

t +48 81 501 41 29
w www.przepioreczka.com.pl

Famously claims to be the town's oldest hotel, now equipped with a curative salt cave that is open for 45-minute sessions that start on the hour. There is a 20 per cent discount on standard prices for hotel guests. A double room costs PLN 250 per night including breakfast.

RIGHT *Lush garden walking trails in Park Zdrojowy.*

shoestring rates – Willa Raj, Willa Brzozy and Willa Feniks allow guests easy booking of interchangeable treatments.

The top-end offering is the red-roofed Willa Raj, a statuesque, white mansion in its own large garden with a natural fish-filled pond. Apartments are simple but cosy at Willa Brzozy while accommodation is hostel-style at Willa Feniks. One of the Spa w Raju's most popular therapies is the detoxifying oxygen microdermabrasion facial, a deep cleanse that helps to eradicate pollutants and toxins from the skin therefore improving cell function and increasing oxygen intake. Other in-demand therapies include anti-cellulite wraps, colon-cleansing treatments and an intensive detoxification treatment.

Modern and Traditional Options

Facilities are equally impressive at the **Willa Monika Spa**, where a state-of-the-art wellness centre has a therapy and treatment menu packed with sublime 90-minute massages using naturally scented oils.

Another much-loved Nałęczów spa hotel is the **Hotel Przepióreczka**, the town's first, and therefore a popular landmark building. Everyone in Nałęczów knows the fine, stone structure, which has been carefully modernized and refurbished in recent years to offer 26 air-conditioned rooms together with a relaxing, restorative salt cave. Comprising a natural mix of largely domestic-mined and maritime salts, the cave's healing environment mixes salty spray with beneficial air humidity, temperature and circulation. The continual release of valuable ions of iodine, magnesium, potassium and bromine can help to ease laboured breathing and hypertension, and soothe itchy skin complaints and blemishes. The salt cave is also open to non-residents for 45-minute sessions, 8am–7pm.

Krynica Zdrój

At an altitude of 560–620m (1,837–2,034ft) above sea level, the mountain wellness retreat of Krynica Zdrój is arguably Poland's most famous spa town.

The town lies 161km (100 miles) south of Kraków in the Carpathian Mountains. The settlement has a wealth of traditional wood and brick architecture, including historic sanatoriums, pump rooms and mudbath centres all based on a series of thermal water wells. Long hailed as a cure for urinary and digestive ailments, the waters of Krynica (meaning 'well' in Slavic) are now bottled and sold under a trio of brand names. The therapeutic mineral waters are why Krynica has been dubbed the 'pearl of Polish spas'.

Taking the Waters

Located on verdant hills along the valley of the Kryniczanka stream, at the eastern end of the Beskid Sądecki mountain range, the spa town's heritage dates back to the 18th century. Today, to stroll along Krynica's handsome indoor promenade with its winter garden and marvellous theatre complex is to wander back in time to the days when nobility would descend upon the town. Guests at the **GeoVita** spa (see below) can frequent the local pump room for a sip of Krynica's 'magic cure-all' under the majestic shadows of the Carpathian Mountain peaks. Ingestion of the waters still plays a central role in the thermal-springs' healing in the town, in conjunction with outdoor recreation along over 160km (99½ miles) of leafy tourist trails for hikes and mountain biking across the mountains to woods, parks and gardens.

Classic and Specialist Treatments

Featuring some of the most famous names in Polish medicine, the GeoVita spa works in close partnership with some of the nation's most prestigious conventional medical centres. It has state-of-the-art health facilities, qualified doctors and a therapy menu of massage, beauty

ABOVE Mountain-biking is a popular activity in the area.

3 things you **must not** miss

1 Skiing Area of Wierchomla
In this area modern facilities and a traditional regional ambience combine to great effect. Fabulous slopes (for skiers of all abilities) hide among the woods close to the picturesque Tysina Creek.
www.wierchomla.com.pl

2 Wooden Architecture Route
From this 1,500-km (932-mile) route you can marvel at 230 of the most significant landmarks in the area – Christian and Orthodox churches, granaries, chapels and manor houses.
www.poland.travel

▶ 3 Dunajec River
From Krynica Zdrój head to the Dunajec River, between Poland and Slovakia, set among beautiful limestone mountains and dramatic water-carved rock formations.
www.krynica.pl

GEOVITA

t +48 18 471 04 00
w www.geovita.pl

Offers guest an impressive range of wellness programmes, including an all-in four-night well-being package including massage, water therapies, drinking cures, cleansing teas and a variety of relaxing pampering treatments, from PLN 950.

HOTEL KRYNICA

t +48 18 473 71 00
w www.hotelkrynica.eu

Overlooking the picturesque, green slopes of the Jaworzyna Mountain, this fine spa hotel specializes in good-quality classic massage and restorative therapies such as full-body mud applications, priced from PLN 90.

ABOVE Neo-Renaissance beauty: The Sanatorium 'Old Spa House'.

treatments and tender-touch therapies as well as offering a specialist range of clinical healthcare disciplines, such as the treatment of neurological complaints, post-natal depression, migraines and obesity.

Attracting international wellness tourists in their droves, the spa at **Hotel Krynica** has built a fine reputation for reliable, good-quality, classic massage therapies using natural balms, herb oils, mountain-plant infusions and hot stones. The massage duration ranges from 30–80 minutes, the latter giving you the ultimate, deep-touch, relaxing treat. The spa has an indoor pool, whirlpool, several saunas, a vapour bath and a fitness studio – all of which are maintained to first-class standards. Menus at the hotel can be adapted by the chef to suit all types of diets, from low fat and salt free to vegetarian, wheat free and macrobiotic. Guests can also choose from a number of spa packages and therapy programmes, including a number of seasonal specials, so be sure to check online.

Wieliczka

In the 18th century, a well-travelled Frenchman observed that the Wieliczka salt mine was no less magnificent than the Egyptian pyramids – and today millions of visitors wholeheartedly agree.

This crystalline, subterranean world of labyrinthine passages, giant caverns, underground lakes and chapels is just 10km (6 miles) from the centre of the city of Kraków. Wieliczka can be reached by one of the many minibuses that run from Kraków's main train station. You can also catch a train to the local town station, which is about a 10-minute taxi ride from the mine.

Mined for 900 years, the salt mine was once the world's biggest and most profitable, as axes, shovels and picks excavated the medieval equivalent of today's oil. In nine centuries of mining, the Wieliczka mine became riddled with large corridors and passages – 200km (124 miles) in all, plus 2,040 caverns gouged out of the shimmering grey-white salt rock. The Kopalnia Soli Wieliczka (Wieliczka Salt Mine) has been granted an International Certificate ISO 9001:2000 for Quality

Management System in Health Protection and is UNESCO-protected via the World Heritage List. At around 10°C (50°F) the mine's climate is crisp and cold. Reaching a depth of 327m (1,073ft), the mine has plenty of surprises with intricate passageways created by mine workers that lead to an elaborate rock-salt cathedral complete with pews, statues of religious deities and chandeliers carved from glassy droplets of reconstituted salt. Constructed over nine levels, the mine is accessed by a wooden stairway of 378 steps.

Underground Treatment Centre

Salt therapies draw wellness tourists to Wieliczka salt mine's deep-rock curative cavern, known as the **Podziemny Ośrodek Rehabilitacyjno-Leczniczy** (Underground Rehabilitation and Treatment Centre) situated in the Lake Wessel Chamber. With a unique microclimate, this unusual health

ABOVE Statue in the salt mine's chapel.

3 things you **must not** miss

1 Outdoor Activities
Although a small and rather industrialized village, Wieliczka is surrounded by picturesque rolling hills, thick forests and occasional streams with plenty of opportunities for hiking, cycling and horse riding.

2 Round of Golf
Head to the curvaceous fairways of the nine-hole Royal Kraków Golf & Country Club in the village of Ochmanów, between Wieliczka and Niepolomice. *www.krakowgolf.pl*

▶ **3 Day Trip to Kraków**
Take a trip into lively Kraków with its buzzing nightlife, neon-lit bars, cafes, restaurants, galleries, museums and theatres – buses depart every hour. *www.krakow.pl*

**PODZIEMNY OŚRODEK
REHABILITACYJNO-
LECZNICZY, KOPALNIA
SOLI WIELICZKA**

t +48 12 278 73 68
w www.sanatorium.
   kopalnia.pl

*Pre-booking is essential.
The 17-day outpatient
package is from PLN 1,880
per person.*

ABOVE Exercise class in the salt mine.

OPPOSITE Wieliczka is surrounded by beautiful countryside.

resort offers a range of treatments, including an array of highly popular programmes. Typically, guests suffer from skin complaints, breathing difficulties or allergies or they may be recovering from illnesses connected to the throat, lungs or sinuses. Salt therapies have also proven highly effective in the treatment of obesity. The core treatment is spending around six hours in an atmosphere noted for its bacteriological purity, laden with sodium chloride, magnesium and calcium ions. Additional therapies supplement this, including massage, laser therapy and cosmetic services.

Salt Treatments

The treatment centre is staffed by qualified health clinicians. Research has found that sodium chloride (salt) is particularly beneficial for health when delivered with negative ions. Called speleotherapy, salt-cave therapy requires a combination of minerals and electronegative charge. Wieliczka's fully illuminated, air-conditioned and ventilated healing chambers have been proven to be beneficial in the treatment of stress, tension, respiratory ailments, allergies, neurosis and depression. Medical consultations and diagnostic tests are part of the programmes as are exercise and other activities. As well as the recommended long-stay therapeutic package, a seven-day wellness option is available, as are night-treatment stays. Many guests feel the healing power of this most unusual microclimate within a few minutes, reporting ease of breathing and a notable calming of acute dermal symptoms. Accommodation is offered in a nearby hotel.

LITHUANIA

travel essentials

TIME DIFFERENCE: GMT +2
TELEPHONE CODE: +370
CURRENCY: Litas
CAPITAL: Vilnius
LANGUAGE: Lithuanian

WHEN TO GO: Spring and summer (May through to September) are warm and sunny, although the mid-summer holiday (in June) sees crowds swell. July and August draw international visitors while many locals are on holiday. Winter (November to March) brings snowfall and only a few hours of daylight each day.

Druskininkai

As the oldest and most popular Lithuanian wellness resort, Druskininkai has a well-developed spa infrastructure with several complexes tucked among the 100-year-old spa pavilions and thermal pumps.

Popular today with nouveau-riche Poles, Russians and Latvians, the town of Druskininkai became famous for its thermal springs in the 19th century, attracting wealthy sophisticates in need of water-based cures. Specializing in bathing and therapeutic mud treatments, Druskininkai is located amid oxygen-rich pine forests, dozens of freshwater lakes and rolling countryside. An absence of industry ensures the town's air is of the highest purity, containing an abundance of negative (light) ions. Breezes off the pollution-free Neman River fan Druskininkai's scenic woodlands, hills and forest reserves, close to the borders with Poland and Belarus, around 130km (81 miles) from Vilnius.

Wellness Renaissance

Renowned throughout Eastern Europe for its salty subterranean wells and warm microclimate, Druskininkai's name comes from the Lithuanian word for salt (*druska*), in honour of the town's salt-rich waters. Other mineral compounds include calcium, potassium, iodine, bromine, iron and magnesium – a powerful blend that prompted Tsar Nicholas I of Russia to bestow spa status on Druskininkai in 1837.

After the uncertainty and troubles of the First World War and the Polish invasion, Druskininkai experienced a meteoritic period of construction in the 1950s as luxurious villas, spa hospitals and sanatoriums were built in the centre of town. During the collapse of the Soviet Union, Druskininkai became neglected and unfashionable until a wellness renaissance in the early 2000s saw a slew of privately owned spas, clinics and healing centres suddenly begin to spring up all over town.

ABOVE *Therapy at Spa Vilnius.*

OPPOSITE *Druskonis Lake.*

3 things you **must not** miss

1 The Devil Stone
Located a few kilometres from Druskininkai, Švendubrė village is renowned for its mystical Devil stone. This jutting, rounded hunk of rock can be reached on foot or by bike via a pretty cycleway and footpath through the forest. *www.info.druskininkai.lt*

2 Neo-Gothic Church
Marvel at the camomile blooms inside the Švš. Mergelės Marijos Škaplierinės Bažnyčia (Holy Virgin Mary Scapular Church), built in 1931. in Druskininkai's historic town centre near the lake.

▶ 3 Family Day Out
Revel in the water slides, pools and fun tubs at the town's state-of-the-art Vandens Parkas (Aqua Park). *www.akvapark.lt*

RIGHT Funky hammam at Spa Vilnius.

OPPOSITE ABOVE Ambient Ayurveda room, Spa Vilnius

OPPOSITE BELOW Charming old spa pavilion by the river.

One particular low-key wellness resort hotel, the **Spa Vilnius SANA**, is far removed from a notion of an austere boot camp, despite being housed in a charmless Soviet-era concrete block. It's definitely more glam than glum. It has successfully taken an example of Druskininkai's dowdy architecture and transformed it with a funky refurbishment that has added plenty of stylish pizzazz.

Spa Vilnius SANA

Every member of the therapy staff at Spa Vilnius is trained to the highest standard, ensuring guests can book with complete peace of mind and then breathe and relax. No need for anxiety here: everything runs like clockwork but not in an overly enthusiastic, bureaucratic way – the pace is measured, smooth and easy. To the sound of classical music, a menu of treatments is delivered in moodily lit therapy suites scented with aromatherapy oils.

Traditional Lithuanian massage is similar to a Swedish and sports massage combined, with strong, firm, deep strokes that pummel, stretch and pound to an up-tempo rhythm. Back, thighs, calves, shoulders and even face, neck, wrists and bust get a serious going over – the results are revitalizing rather than relaxing, with your skin is left pink and perky.

Druskininkai's thick, black healing mud contains dense peat deposits and at Spa Vilnius it is used in baths, wraps and facials. Big chunks of ancient plant-life have mulched down to sodden clumps of decaying sediment and it is these that are hailed for their miraculous properties and far-reaching health benefits.

Harvested from local boggy fields, the mud is mixed into a rough paste and then applied to the skin, to which it sticks in dollops. Due to its lengthy period of decomposition without oxygen on the marshes, all of the mud's vegetative organisms are rich in microbiological matter at the point of harvest.

Unlike many ultra-swish Western spas, you'll see lots of potions and lotions in plain bottles at the Spa Vilnius.

Vessels that contain Druskininkai's slightly mineralized elixir are everywhere for anyone who fancies a passing swig. At Spa Vilnius, ingestion therapies are mainly aimed at those keen to shed a few pounds, reduce stress and generally nurture their bodies.

Programmes are more intensive at the nearby **Eglės Sanatorija**, where over 1,000 guests per day are treated with a smorgasbord of thermal-water inhalations, massages, colonic irrigation, salt-based remedies and bubbling therapeutic iodine-bromine-*Sūrutis* baths. They also offer a number of programmes for those with a specific goal in mind, such as weight loss.

INFORMATION

SPA VILNIUS SANA
t +370 313 53 811
w www.spa-vilnius.lt

Prepare to be dazzled by an intoxicating array of sumptuous therapies with de luxe full-body massages from 129 LT. Born in summer? Mention this when booking to receive a special gift!

EGLĖS SANATORIJA
t +370 313 60 220
w www.sanatorija.lt

Ring for tailored pricing for a wide range of mineral and herb therapies and dedicated wellness programmes. Online discounts are available, together with special packages. A mineral mudbath costs from 25 LT.

LATVIA

travel essentials

TIME DIFFERENCE: GMT +2

TELEPHONE CODE: +371

CURRENCY: Lats

CAPITAL: Riga

LANGUAGE: Latvian

WHEN TO GO: Latvia's prime tourist season runs from April to September, with July and August the most crowded months. Midsummer is highly popular with domestic tourists, so accommodation needs to be booked in advance.

Jūrmala

In Latvia's major spa town, Jūrmala, birch sap has featured as a common ingredient in facial creams, lotions, cleansers and emulsions for over 150 years.

In the historic seaside town of Jūrmala, a 40-minute drive from Riga, well-being has been at the forefront of tourism since the Soviet era. Wedged between the Gulf of Riga and the Lielupe River, Jūrmala is famous for its 33-km (20½-mile) stretch of scenic, bone-white sands, art nouveau architecture, health resorts and pretty wooden houses. In the late 18th and early 19th centuries, Jūrmala's reputation as a spa destination began to take hold when it started to attract affluent landowners seeking coastal relaxation. Russian army officers then came here to rest after the Napoleonic Wars and the resort became a firm favourite with the high-ranking communist elite.

Here, Latvian birch sap has been used as a cure-all for centuries and is extracted from the trees in early spring. To Latvians, birch sap is the drink of the gods, an elixir of life and a health-giving power drink. Served slightly sweet as a welcome to visitors and a salutary gesture to good health, this all-natural tonic is consumed to combat everything from exhaustion and post-winter blues to scurvy, gout, kidney pain and rickets. When fermented, the nation's traditional homespun tipple becomes a potent vodka-like liquor that is said to have antiseptic, anti-parasitic, anti-inflammatory and anti-itching properties. Rich in amino acids and proteins, each swig also bursts with vitamin C, potassium, calcium, magnesium and zinc. When combined with organic oils and applied to the skin it also acts as a highly effective hydrating therapy, helping to restore skin tone and the suppleness lost through exposure to Latvia's harsh, cold winter weather.

Birch Sap Therapies

Many of Jūrmala's main spas use birch sap and indigenous herbs as part of weight-loss programmes. The detoxifying wraps at the

ABOVE Birch tree grove near the town.

OPPOSITE Example of a typical house in Jūrmala.

3 things you **must not** miss

1 Town Stroll
Enjoy a scenic stroll along Jūrmala's handsome central promenade, Jomas iela. Admire the old wooden houses nestled among boutiques, parks and plazas. *www.visitjurmala.com*

2 Sun, Sea and Sand
Relax on Jūrmala's stretch of powder-fine white sand backed by attractive forests and woodlands. The clean, shallow, calm waters are ideal for swimming under sunny skies. *www.visitjurmala.com*

▶ **3 Day Trip to Riga**
Riga is a 30-minute drive from Jūrmala. Revel in the jaw-dropping views of the Riga skyline from the Akmens Bridge. *www.rigatourism.lv*

BALTIC BEACH HOTEL

t +371 6777 1446

w www.balticbeach.lv

*A full-day restorative
Nature's Energy
programme, which includes
herbal soaks, mud wraps,
healing birch tea and a
shoreline walk, is 49 LVL.*

**AMBER SEA HOTEL
AND SPA**

t + 371 6775 1297

w www.amberhotel.lv

*Set among aromatic pine
trees with the sound of the
waves in the background,
try the Forever Young
therapy to experience the
rejuvenating power of
indigenous wild plants and
herbs, including a variety of
mosses and birch at their
best (70 LVL).*

ALVE SPA HOTEL

t +371 6775 5970

w www.alve.lv

*Set on a dune sea-coast
landscape, this curative spa
draws on the fresh sea air as
a natural body vitalizer. Full-
day pampering sessions
including a massage with
essential oils, Latvian plants,
wildflowers and birch from
115 LVL.*

RIGHT *Crowd-free sands
close to the Amber Sea Hotel
and Spa.*

spa at the **Baltic Beach Hotel** and **Amber Sea Hotel and Spa** are an education in plant power. The anti-cellulite therapies at the **Alve Spa Hotel** are very popular. As an exfoliating scrub, birch sap is often combined with crushed seeds or fruit husks and fennel to provide a rough-textured paste that polishes the skin's outer layer. Birch twigs and bark are also added to hot, healing mudbaths to provide a fresher, more relaxing aroma.

Local Liquor

And after a Latvian all-natural health-giving massage? What better way to unwind further than with a glass of birch-sap wine infused with juniper berries – an ancient health-giving tipple made from boiled, fresh juice sprinkled with dried fruit. Once fermented, it's then bottled and stored for at least a month for a delectable medium-dry flavour. But be warned, many swear that this drink boosts fertility, so sip with caution!

ESTONIA

travel essentials

TIME ZONE: GMT +2

TELEPHONE CODE: +372

CURRENCY: Estonian Kroon

CAPITAL: Tallinn

LANGUAGE: Estonian

WHEN TO GO: Estonia's temperate climate is characterized by warm summers and fairly severe winters, with year-round breezes from the Baltic Sea. Summer temperatures average 21°C (70°F) with July the hottest month. Winters can be severe with temperatures of -8°C (18°F) on average, although drops to -23°C (-9°F) aren't uncommon.

Tallinn

In Tallinn's quaint, medieval Old Town signposts for 'Sauna Tower' and 'Sauna Street' are testament to the importance of the humble sweat-bath to daily life.

ABOVE *Saunas provide the ultimate deep-cleanse.*

OPPOSITE *St Alexander Nevsky Cathedral, Tallinn.*

PREVIOUS PAGE *View of Tallinn.*

As an intrinsic part of modern culture, from courtship, friendship and networking to well-being and matrimony, the sauna is central to Estonian bonding, pondering and unity. After a long, dark, bone-chilling snowy winter it is also a great way to thaw out. Estonia's saunas fulfil a variety of functions, depending on who you ask. Some say they are merely a way to keep clean, others that they are an unbeatable hangover cure. Many believe saunas are vital to a healthy sex life and matters of the heart. Others that they help promote a deep, restful sleep. Yet every Estonian is in agreement on three things – a sauna is a crucial part of maintaining good health, aiding longevity and is a truly unbeatable way to relax.

Cleanse, Steam and Sizzle

As you'd expect in a metropolis, the sauna experiences are varied, ranging from rustic age-old traditional establishments to venues that are much more swish. Tallinn's oldest sauna baths, **Kalma Saun**, built in 1928, still retains plenty of old-fashioned neighbourhood charm that hasn't been compromised by modern additions. A sociable atmosphere centres on male- and female-only saunas and sauna traditions that date back around 700 years.

First, you take a cleansing shower, then grab a spot on the sauna's hot wooden seat (bring a towel so that your rump doesn't sizzle when you sit down as the thermometer will soar past 95°C (203°F)). By scooping water from a bucket (*leil*) and pouring it on to the hot stones the heat will rise, prompting a flow of perspiration to drenching point. Next, refresh with an icy shower before rejoining your hot and sweaty companions for a second sitting. Private saunas can be rented by groups (mixed genders allowed). After an invigorating rub to help rid the body of toxins 'loosened' by the heat, honey is traditionally rubbed into

3 things you **must not** miss

◀ 1 Cycle Ride
Hire a bicycle to explore Lahemaa, a peaceful national park east of Tallinn that is home to historic manor houses, seaside villages and natural beauty.
www.lahemaa.ee and *www.citybike.ee*

2 Natural History Museum
Learn about the living things that can be found in the Estonian outdoors at the Loodusmuuseum (National History Museum).
www.loodusmuuseum.ee

3 Life Behind Bars
The Soviet-era Patarei Prison, a gloomy fortress surrounded by guard towers and barbed wire, left virtually untouched since it closed in 2004, is now open to the public and is one of the city's quirkier attractions.
www.tourism.tallinn.ee

Yield to the traditional, wholesome health benefits of an authentic, olden-style sauna at this 83-year-old facility where rituals remain unchanged by time. Costs 95–130 EEK per person. Open 10am–11pm.

Opt for a deluxe, 30-minute honey massage therapy (400 EEK) after a session in one of the spa's private saunas (75 EEK per person), with the largest VIP sauna suite big enough for 15 of your close personal friends.

the skin as a natural moisturizer and a sweet-smelling sticky finale (though it is more common nowadays for therapists to use a honey-based moisturizer).

High-end Heat

In contrast, the ultra-modern **Kalev Spa** is a well-appointed wellness centre offering top-end luxury spa therapies complemented by a state-of-the-art suite of saunas, with a shower room, bubble bath, steam room and special sauna menu. After 30 minutes in the infrared sauna, opt for a detoxifying wrap or an hour-long traditional Estonian firm-pressure massage followed by a restorative jug of Viru Valge vodka, the nation's clear and light homespun tipple – and the perfect après sauna treat.

ABOVE Sauna therapies are central to good health at the Kalma Saun.

RIGHT Sauna Street – honouring Tallinn's lengthy sauna tradition.

RUSSIA

travel essentials

TIME ZONE: GMT +2 / GMT +3

TELEPHONE CODE: +7

CURRENCY: Rouble

CAPITAL: Moscow

LANGUAGE: Russian

WHEN TO GO: Russia's humid continental European climate turns subarctic in Siberia and to tundra in the polar north. Summers vary from hot, dry and sunny to cool and breezy along the Arctic coast, with sticky city microclimates and windblown rural expanses.

St Petersburg

Rich wines, fine gastronomy and a highly developed cultural scene combine in an artistic city where, put simply, only the very best will do.

ABOVE Caviar facial – decadent, mineral-rich nourishment.

OPPOSITE Church of our Saviour on the Spilled Blood, St Petersburg.

PREVIOUS PAGE State Hermitage Museum, St Petersburg.

In resplendent St Petersburg a well-heeled population revel in a magical architectural jigsaw of poetic glided domes, ornate fairytale towers, bejewelled historic opulence and palatial mansions. Late-baroque piles in blue, red, gold and green have 'whipped cream' stucco facades adorned with grandiose frescoes and precious inlaid motifs. Guarding the mouth of the Neva River, St Petersburg evokes romance, art, passion and spirit above a thread of waterways and canals.

Caviar Cure

It seems the rest of the world is slowly waking up to what the Russians have known since the era of Catherine the Great: that one of the greatest aids to replenishing skin is a healthy dollop of fish eggs. With its highly concentrated source of nutrients, just a tiny serving of caviar is packed with vitamins. It also helps promote untold smoothness and elasticity when slathered on the skin. As Russia's beloved national delicacy, caviar is harvested from the Caspian Sea and is available in a trio of varieties: beluga, osetra and sevruga. Considered a status symbol, cure-all, hangover remedy, aphrodisiac and brain-power agent, thousands of tonnes of caviar are consumed in St Petersburg each year. Across the city, caviar's role in well-being therapies reflects its synonymy with decadent luxury. Attracting the world's moneyed elite with a promise of the secret of eternal youth, caviar penetrates deep into the pores to provide sublime mega-nourishment for older skin with goo so light it doesn't clog the dermal layers.

Luxury Treatments

According to skin gurus at the swanky new **Astoria Spa** at the Hotel Astoria, caviar has a cell structure very similar to human collagen. Therapies begin with a thorough cleansing, followed by a fruit-enzyme peel,

3 things you **must not** miss

◀ 1 Boat Tour
Take a boat tour of the city, many of which start from the Winter Palace. *www.russian-cruises.ru*

2 On Foot or by Bicycle
Explore St Petersburg on foot or bicycle, from early-morning strolls to ambling pub crawls, ghost walks and cultural tours. *www.peterswalk.com*

3 Vodka Museum
The museum conducts guided tours during which you will hear about vodka's origin, Russian dining traditions and the connection between the history of the Russian state and this drink. *www.vodkamuseum.su*

ASTORIA SPA, HOTEL ASTORIA

t +7 812 494 5757
w www.thehotelastoria.com

Deluge your dermal layers with the rich, nutrient-laden healing properties of Russian fish eggs at the ritzy seventh-floor spa where an afternoon Caviar Delight pampering package (around 3,000 RUB) includes an evening of tasting top-notch caviar.

RELAXATION CENTRE, KEMPINSKI HOTEL MOIKA 22

t +7 812 335 9111
w www.kempinski.com

Rich in historic imperial style that oozes sophistication, the Relaxation Centre's cleansing mineral wraps, sauna, bathing and massages come with panoramic city views – stunning. A nourishing facial costs around 2,300 RUB.

PLANET HEALTH CLUB AND BEAUTY ROOM, GRAND HOTEL EUROPE

t +7 812 329 6597
w www.grandhotel europe.com

This fine hotel upholds a proud hospitality tradition with a swish, well-equipped well-being centre where body wraps, massages and scrubs with moisturizing facials start at 3,000 RUB.

ABOVE *The swish Hotel Astoria.*

then the skin is cleaned again using warm bursts of steam. Next, a thick green paste containing sevruga extracts is applied to the skin in saturating quantities with a trowel, as you relax, rather fittingly, to the soothing sounds of the sea. After around 20 minutes you're gently roused from a fishy slumber for a gentle facial massage that sets the exotic little salty morsels off to work. A moisturizing lotion laden with caviar nutrients further feeds the skin to leave it plumped up, with facial lines diminished. This Russian superfood adds a suppleness that seems to come from the lower layers of the skin to help lessen sagging. Softer,

tighter skin glows with a youthful tone that comes from caviar's ability to encourage dormant cells to regenerate. St Petersburg's signature caviar facial has fast become all the rage with visiting culture lovers keen to experience the ultimate reviving therapy after a day trawling palaces and museums.

At both the **Relaxation Centre** at the Kempinski Hotel Moika 22 and the **Planet Health Club and Beauty Room** at the Grand Hotel Europe, tiny dishes of fine sevruga are served to guests awaiting the tender care of their therapists – often with a fortifying glass of vodka on the side in the style of tsars, nobility and oligarchs.

Caucasus Mountains

The claim by advocates of colonic cleansing that it aids longevity appears to be borne out by the people of the Caucasus Mountains, who famously enjoy long and healthy lives.

ABOVE *Autumn in Pyatigorsk.*

In many societies, the subject of colon cleansing isn't considered a standard topic of daily conversation. This is not so in rural Russia, where a healthy digestive tract has long been viewed as fundamental to good health and well-being. It was Russian Nobel Prize-winning microbiologist Ilya Ilyich Mechnikov's (1845–1916) theory, that the build-up of colonic toxins resulted in a shorter life expectancy, which led to a sweeping wave of irrigation therapies Russia-wide. By the late 19th century, intestinal cleansing had become a fundamental part of Russia's health practices as a greater awareness of the potential ills associated with constipation, excess toxins and colonic congestion took hold.

Regional Health Tradition

Many inhabitants of the Caucasus Mountains wellness region assert to lifespans of 150 years, marriages at 110 and claims of fatherhood at 136. Certainly the local Abkhazia people are considerably fitter and healthier than most of the rest of the population of Europe – running up and down the mountains, laughing and dancing well into later life with no signs of chronic illness. Favouring a wholesome, high-fibre diet and regular enemas, the communities of the Caucasus Mountains also ingest milky-white brackish spring waters that rise up from the depths of the earth at an altitude of 2,591–4,267m (8,500–14,000ft). This milky-white water sustains many villages in the region's sheltered mountain valleys amid fertile lakes and woods.

Today, numerous spas in the Caucasus Mountains wellness region specialize in naturopathic therapies that place digestive-tract cleansing, enemas and colonic irrigation to the fore.

Wellness Region

In the southern town of Zheleznovodsk, colonic cleansing is a mainstay of dozens of

3 things you **must not** miss

1 Take to the Air
Gliding among the peaks, valleys, canyons, waterfalls and lakes of the picturesque Caucasus Mountains is an exhilarating experience. Glider planes, hang-gliding and heli-gliding are all popular in this region. *www.glidingsport.ru*

2 Forest Climb
Meaning 'Five Mountains', Pyatigorsk is a great departure point for numerous hiking routes. Visit the following website for day trip and excursion options. *www.tour-life.com*

▶ 3 Riverside Picnic
Join picnicking families along Pyatigorsk's scenic Podkumok River in summer for barbecue parties, swimming, music and dance. *www.pyatigorsk.org*

INFORMATION

MASHUK-AKVA TERM SPA

w www.mashuk-akvaterm.ru

A two-night gastroenterology treatment package starts at 6,725 RUB per person.

PYATIGORSK RESEARCH INSTITUTE OF BALNEOLOGY AND PHYSIOTHERAPY CLINIC

w www.pyat.ru/eng-main.htm

Healing dips in the therapeutic mineral-rich waters are priced from 935 RUB.

BELOW *Historic hydropathic building in Pyatigorsk.*

health spas that use water drawn from the local mineral spring sources in the pursuit of long life through rectal health. Around 60 litres (13 gallons) of pure, filtered water are used per treatment, but only small amounts are allowed to enter the bowel – and the vast majority comes out again. Part of the therapy is a gentle stomach massage that works around the whole bowel to assist with the elimination of waste and gas pockets – sometimes herbal infusions are used with a probiotic (friendly bacteria) implant administered occasionally during the 45-minute cleanse.

At the **Mashuk-Akva Term Spa** in Zheleznovodsk, a team of fully qualified hydrotherapists and enema specialists are proud of their region's health tradition – so much so that they erected a 1.5-m (5-ft) bronze sculpture in honour of the anal syringe.

The Mashuk-Akva Spa believes that cleansing the colon is as normal, hygienic and essential as brushing your teeth. Once impacted material is removed, the colon can begin working again. In this sense colonic cleansing using thermal water is a rejuvenation treatment and certainly one that has a loyal following in Russia's Caucasus Mountain wellness region.

Aside from the well-known Mashuk-Akva Term Spa the region has a number of other notable institutions, including the **Pyatigorsk Research Institute of Balneology and Physiotherapy Clinic**, a well-respected health resort that uses the local waters in a comprehensive range of therapies, including several purgative delights. The town of Pyatigorsk is stretched on the slopes of the Mashuk Mountain where 40 mineral springs have been discovered.

HUNGARY

travel essentials

TIME ZONE: GMT +1

TELEPHONE CODE: +36

CURRENCY: Forint

CAPITAL: Budapest

LANGUAGE: Hungarian

WHEN TO GO: Hungary is characterized by warm, dry summers and fairly cold winters, with January the coldest month. May–September is mild and pleasant with cool nights and comfortable day time temperatures. October to December is chilly and wet, sometimes snowy. January and February are subject to snowfall, especially in the mountainous regions.

Budapest

Budapest, Hungary's history-rich principal city, has the distinction of being the world's great 'Spa Capital', as it is the only capital city with authentic thermal boreholes inside its urban mass.

ABOVE Bathe in splendour at the Gellért Thermal Baths.

OPPOSITE The gardens and front entrance of the Széchenyi Thermal Baths.

PREVIOUS PAGE View of Budapest.

After Iceland, Hungary has the world's largest thermal water resources, with over 80 per cent of its land mass richly endowed with hot medicinal springs. Beneath the historic metropolis of Budapest lies a gurgling riddle of hundreds of fast-flowing medicinal streams and boreholes dating back over 2,000 years. Deep subterranean limestone caverns containing vast water resources reach temperatures of up to 73°C (163°F). These bubbling groundwater wells carry around two million bathtubs of water per day.

Budapest residents have believed in the therapeutic benefits of their subterranean springs since Celtic tribes settled the area – and much of the population has been stripping and dipping ever since. The 100 freshwater wells that pump healing waters through the veins of Budapest fill around 50 spas, pools and bathhouses – as well as numerous siphons for ingested medicinal drinking cures. As a hotbed of

scalding geothermal activity, Budapest owes much of its modern bathing culture to a 150-year period of Turkish rule during the 16th and 17th centuries. Frequented by every social class, from Budapesti aristocrats to shop assistants, the baths became a gathering point for informal meetings, gossip and gentle healing – and nothing much has changed.

Historic Bathhouses

Built in 1565, the **Király Gyógyfürdö** (Király Thermal Baths) date back to the time of Turkish rule, with a resplendent cupola-topped pool an architectural highlight. Four pools filled with medicinal water from the same pump as the nearby Lukács Gyógyfürdö és Uszoda (Király is the only bathhouse without its own spring) offer temperatures of 26°, 32°, 36° and 40°C (80°, 90°, 103°, 104°F). First, there is a hot-air chamber, fired up to encourage a rise in

3 things you **must not** miss

◀ 1 City Oasis
Beautiful Margit-sziget (Margaret's Island) is the city's green oasis, with its romantic walkways, medieval ruins, fountains, swimming pools and trails through gardens of gorgeous foliage.
www.budapestinfo.hu

2 Sample Hungarian Wines
The Magyar Borok Háza (House of Hungarian Wines) is located in the historic milieu of the Castle District of Buda. There are over 700 Hungarian wines from each of Hungary's 22 wine-producing regions.
www.budapestinfo.hu

3 Free Walking Tours
Free entertaining daily walks – one day on the Buda side, the other on the Pest.
www.budapestinfo.hu

body temperature. A narrow entrance leads to the dome itself, where deep niches under the vaults support the cupola. The octagonal layout is small and compact with a trio of small pools representing the hottest and coldest of the four. Benches trim the main pool, but can often barely be seen through the shroud of thick steam and tiny shafts of light shining in through pinprick holes in the cupola. Most visitors bob around in the water, eyes closed, absorbing the gentle murmur in the dimness. After bathing, the hammam beckons – it is even darker and steamier than the main pool but is partially illuminated by flickering lamps.

Perfectly located in the heart of the city, **Rudas Gyógyfürdö és Uszoda** (Rudas Thermal Baths) occupy a skinny strip of land between Gellért Hill and the River Danube. Providing an outstanding example of architecture dating from the Turkish period, the trademark octagonal pool takes centre stage, framed by a striking 9-m

(30-ft) diameter cupola and eight towering pillars. As the more boisterous of Budapest's bathing houses, the Rudas is popular with a younger crowd, staying open till the small hours at weekends when it stages lively party nights. However, during daylight hours the mood is mellow and magical in this most grand setting. Six thermal wellness pools run from 16–42°C (61–108°F). Prior to 2005 this had been a male-only environment since 1966. Today, it is open for mixed-gender, women-only and men-only bathing sessions. Bath-side massages are offered by a strong-handed Hungarian masseuse in small sectioned-off rooms. Other therapies include a full balneotherapy menu, from underwater jet massages and physiotherapy to medicinal carbon-rich dips.

Built in 1918 on the site of a Turkish bath, the **Gellért Gyógyfürdö és Uszoda** (Gellért Thermal Baths) are famous throughout Europe for their immaculately preserved art

INFORMATION

· ·

For more information on all of the bathhouses listed below visit www.budapest gyogyfurdoi.hu

KIRÁLY GYÓGYFÜRDÖ

t +36 1 202 3688

Entrance fee 2,200 HUF.

RUDAS GYÓGYFÜRDÖ ÉS USZODA

t +36 1 356 1322

Prices vary according to the day of the week and time of day; an adult thermal ticket on a weekday is 2,800 HUF.

GELLÉRT GYÓGYFÜRDÖ ÉS USZODA

t +36 1 466 6166

Prices vary according to the day of the week and time of day; an adult thermal ticket on a weekday is 3,600 HUF.

LUKÁCS GYÓGYFÜRDÖ ÉS USZODA

t +36 1 326 1695

Entrance fee on a weekday is 2,500 HUF.

SZÉCHENYI GYÓGYFÜRDÖ ÉS USZODA

t +36 1 363 3210

Entrance fee on a weekday is 3,100 HUF.

nouveau interior. To enter is to experience a world of architectural splendour adorned with fine mosaics in coral, copper and blue hues, marble columns, bright stained-glass windows and statues that make it, without doubt, Budapest's most beautiful bathing complex. Some thirteen mineral boreholes supply the nine pools of the Gellért Baths, with thermal waters at temperatures varying between 27° and 48°C (81° and 118°F).

Though Turkish in origin, the **Lukács Gyógyfürdö és Uszoda** (Lukács Thermal Baths) were popularized at the end of the 19th century when a wellness centre was added to extend its curative menu. Built around an elegant inner courtyard scattered with marble tablets, and once the haunt of intellectuals and artists, the Lukács were the largest of Budapest's thermal baths until the completion of the Széchenyi Baths in 1894. Eight pools offer separate bathing areas for men and women, and there is a large pool equipped with underwater jets,

neck shower, water-beam back massage, whirlpools, geysers and hot tubs. Outside, a cluster of 100-year-old trees provide a relaxing area for a quick nap.

As one of Europe's biggest medicinal bathing complexes, the **Széchenyi Gyógyfürdö és Uszoda** (Széchenyi Thermal Baths) offer neo-baroque grandeur dating back to 1913. Drawing architectural influences from the Romans, the largest pool in this fine golden building is surrounded by smaller tubs filled with curative waters. A 914-m (3,000-ft) drinking well holds water used for the treatment of gastric conditions and kidney complaints. A scenic trio of outdoor pools are open year-round to offer warm-water bathing throughout winter. Ten separate pools and a whole host of natural wellness therapies are available in a therapy zone inside where pampering centres on weight loss, anti-cellulite and anti-ageing treatments, together with skin-softening therapies and physiotherapy.

Lake Balaton and Hévíz

A cluster of spa centres around Lake Balaton offer wellness pilgrims organized programmes of mud-based health therapies combined with oxygen-rich air and warm thermal waters.

ABOVE Garden Fun Bath at the Danubius Health Spa Resort Hévíz.

OPPOSITE ABOVE Whirlpool at the Danubius Health Spa Resort Hévíz.

OPPOSITE BELOW Lido at Lake Balaton.

Lake Balaton

As the largest shallow-water lake in Central Europe, Lake Balaton is unique in that it has a matchless hydrological composition that reflects its extraordinary genesis and evolution. Once a small string of clear, shallow ponds, Lake Balaton has expanded over many centuries to become the so-called 'Hungarian Sea', stretching over 5ha (12 acres). Spring-fed, thermal and naturally renewed every 72 hours at temperatures of 24–38°C (75–100°F), the lake is an example of an eco-healthy expanse rich in nutrients and minerals. It is its 4-m (13-ft) layer of clayey calcareous peat-rich mud that has brought the lake considerable repute since the prehistoric era. Composed of decayed plants, sandy silt, organic matter, shell particles, aqueous vegetation, mineralogical marine deposits, carbonates, water lilies, radioactivity and phosphorous compounds, the mud has been harvested since around 6000 BC. The unique chemical composition of the lake, its temperature, gentle movements and phytoplankton have sustained this organic matter and water mass rich in living organisms without it eroding into a weed-choked, stagnant mess.

Once the curative possibilities of the mud became fully realized and organized by some of Hungary's most respected practitioners, the benefits for patients were clear. As a particularly deep-penetrating organic matter it is believed to be effective in purifying toxins, banishing cellulite, renewing skin cells and deep-cleansing the skin while combating the signs of stress. It was approved as a 'curative' by the Hungarian Ministry of Health in 1956.

Hévíz

Hévíz is a resort town on the flat southern shore of Lake Balaton. One of the most respected wellness establishments here is the four-star **Danubius Health Spa Resort Hévíz**. Located just 500m (546yd) from the

3 things you **must not** miss

◀ 1 Explore on Horseback
Go horse riding along wildlife-rich trails around the lake and explore the surrounding area. *t +36 83 340 851*

2 Local Wine Cellar
Visit the well-stocked Vilmos Cellar, which belongs to the William's Haus apartment complex, to taste local wine vintages. *www.williams haus.hu*

3 Escape on Two Wheels
Most hotels provide or will arrange bicycle hire. Explore the beautiful cycle paths and take the opportunity to complement your spa therapies with some exercise.

shores of the lake and set among lush vegetation, the hotel contains an expansive series of wellness suites, bathing areas and consultation rooms plus a hydropool complete with relaxing underwater music and calm-inducing light effects. A duo of indoor thermal baths are complemented by an outdoor thermal pool, whirlpool, steam room, hot-air bath and indoor and outdoor sauna. A full programme of massage therapies focus on traditional Hungarian deep-tissue-style treatments. These are often combined with hot-mud therapies for the ultimate Lake Balaton wellness splurge, with generous amounts of steaming, thick sludge applied to the body's major joint areas for around 40 minutes until rivers of perspiration flow and toxins begin to release.

At the more intimate three-star **Hotel Erzsébet** the wellness centre is impressive despite its modest size. Therapy menus focus on the radon content of the thermal waters, with a full range of traditional Hévíz natural treatments, from mud wraps to

therapeutic massages, including shiatsu, Ayurveda and Yumeiho. A fully qualified medical staff is focused on illness prevention, with nutrition counselling, weight-control therapies and obesity consultations available. This elegant hotel is popular with wellness tourists seeking revitalization and detoxification treatments. Check the website as there are usually special offers available.

INFORMATION

DANUBIUS HEALTH SPA RESORT HÉVÍZ
t +36 83 889 400
w www.danubiushotels.com

Opt for the signature healing 20-minute mud-wrap therapies in all their hot, sticky, sludgy glory for cleansed, pink, glowing, blemish-free, detoxified skin (16,880 HUF).

HOTEL ERZSÉBET
t +36 83 342 035
w www.erzsebethotel heviz.hu

The wellness centre offers rest and relaxation therapies, from saunas, steam baths, whirlpools and massage to mud-rich facials, from 14,000 HUF.

SLOVENIA

travel essentials

TIME ZONE: GMT +1

TELEPHONE CODE: +386

CURRENCY: Euro

CAPITAL: Ljubljana

LANGUAGE: Slovene

WHEN TO GO: Slovenia's varied climate runs from a continental weather pattern in the north-east and a harsh alpine climate in the mountains to a sub-Mediterranean climate on the coast. For walkers and hikers, April–June offers a colourful wildflower scene-scape as well as inexpensive prices. Both are gone by the time a dry, hot summer arrives, while pleasant autumns can often bring fog and snow by mid-October.

Rogaška Slatina

As the oldest spa resort in Slovenia, Rogaška Slatina confidently entered the 21st century offering anti-stress therapies, anti-ageing techniques and yoga to a new breed of wellness tourist.

Once Rogaška Slatina's waters began surging up through deep, rocky crevices, a hastily erected bottling plant took care of capturing the soon-to-be-famous liquid to prepare it for dispatch and sale across the globe. As a sought-after saleable commodity, these healing waters proved to be a phenomenal success – both as a pick-me-up tonic and a medicine for gastric and digestive ailments. By 1869, 'Rogaška' was one of the world's biggest-selling bottled mineral water (after Vichy and Selters) and with the advent of the railway line from Vienna to Trieste towards the end of the 19th century, the spa proliferated even further, drawing visitors from as far afield as Turkey, Egypt, Tunisia and the USA.

Centuries-old Natural Healing

Today Rogaška Slatina continues to claim its place as one of Slovenia's most important health resorts. Scientific analysis has attested to the therapeutic properties of the local spring waters and these pure, sparkling sources, enriched with high levels of magnesium, remain wholly different to any others found in Slovenia. Rogaška Slatina mixes old-fashioned Slovenian bathing and ingestion therapies with comparatively modern massage techniques and stress-busting programmes.

That Rogaška Slatina's well-being rituals have survived millennia to remain an important part of everyday life – in physical, social, emotional and spiritual terms – is testament to its relevance. People still travel from far and wide to revel in the historic wellness traditions of the town, which enjoys a truly resplendent scenic setting with bloom-filled parks, gardens and mature trees. The grand facades of prestigious old spa hotels and fine contemporary buildings are set against a backdrop of the magnificent verdant slopes of the Kozjansko Hills.

ABOVE Park pavilion, Grand Hotel Sava.

OPPOSITE Park at the Grand Hotel Sava.

3 things you **must not** miss

1 Appreciate Your Surroundings
Pack a pair of binoculars to absorb the striking views of the surrounding lush, green, forested countryside with its colourful blooms, streams, peaks and valleys accessible by numerous man-made paths.

2 Kregar Wine Cellar
Taste your way around this prestigious cellar, frequented by the Viennese Court and guests of Rogaška Slatina's spas since 1860. Tastings are led by a professional sommelier, pre-booking essential (via your hotel). *www.kletkregar.com*

▶ **3 Castle Day Trip**
Enjoy an excursion to the historic castles in Otočec and Ptuj, a fairytale landscape just an hour's drive from Rogaška Slatina town centre. *www.slovenia.info*

Spa Options

In the ultra-plush **Grand Hotel Sava**, native curative plants, medicinal herbs and aromatic shrubs are a strong presence in a staggering array of showers, steam inhalations, lotions, baths, creams, body scrubs and nourishing emulsions. Attracting its fair share of A-list starlets and celebrities, the hotel's modern Lotus Spa is especially proud of its variety of relaxing massages, using a mix of ayurveda, aromatherapy, Slovenian and Thai techniques in combination with traditional relaxing rituals.

Facilities are similarly impressive at the spa at the **Hotel Slovenija**, a fine building in the town's historic quarter built by famous Slovenian architect Jože Plečnik. Characterized by columns and a grand facade, this is a good-value de luxe option. Guests at the hotel can use the state-of-the-art leisure amenities at the nearby Riviera Rogaška complex. Pampering offered by the hotel itself is of a good standard in a well-equipped, spacious spa suite complete with saunas, whirlpools and therapy centre.

Yet it is probably the wellness centre at the swish **Grand Hotel Donat** that caters best for visitors keen to enhance their general well-being. Choose from day packages or spa programmes with accommodation included. There is an eye-popping choice of two-day options packed with relaxation sessions, meditation, traditional bathing, herbal massages and carefully balanced nutritional meals.

INFORMATION

GRAND HOTEL SAVA
t +386 3 811 4000
w www.rogaska.si

Try the seven-day Magnesium Health Programme for a complete pampering experience, from baths and inhalations to yoga and relaxation plus lots of country walks in the mountains, €459.

HOTEL SLOVENIJA
t +386 5 692 9001
w www.lifeclass.net

With prices from €60 per night, including use of spa and recreation facilities, this de luxe hotel is excellent value for money. On site massages from €35.

GRAND HOTEL DONAT
t +386 3 811 3719
w www.ghdonat.com

Two-day well-being packages start at €163 for a comprehensive programme of pampering, relaxation, contemplation and nutrition at this modern hillside spa hotel.

LEFT Grand Hotel Sava's mineral-laden thermal waters.

ABOVE Panoramic view of Grand Hotel Sava.

OPPOSITE Bathing pools at the Grand Hotel Donat.

Dolenjske Toplice

Traditional health cures using curative waters have a long-standing history in this spa resort, where modern bathing rituals continue to draw on age-old traditions.

ABOVE Hotel Vital is famous for its aquatherapy.

OPPOSITE Pools and bathing zones at the Wellness Center Balnea.

Dolenjske Toplice is the earliest mentioned spa town in Slovenian history, with documents attesting to its healing draw dating back to 1228. Half a millennium later, in 1776, the Hotel Vital was built here, followed in 1899 by the Hotel Kristal – both of which are still open today. Situated near the town of Novo Mesto, Dolenjske Toplice is situated in the Dolenjska region on the River Sušica.

Town Development

This lush, natural terrain remains largely unspoiled amid low vineyard-covered hills scattered with wine-growers' cottages and thermal springs. Mineralized waters gush forth at temperatures of 37–38°C (99–100°F) in Dolenjske Toplice, prompting rumours to circulate across Europe in the early 19th century regarding the town's powerful 'wonder waters'.

After the Second World War, the town's bathing therapies extended to better cater for rehabilitation, a therapeutic development that continues to this day. In response to people's need in the modern world for restorative relaxation, time, space and quiet, Dolenjske Toplice has added new wellness facilities and spa complexes to its existing thermal centres. Tailored to meet the needs of modern wellness tourists, old philosophies are now mixed with 21st-century health concepts to help treat anxiety, stress, depression, obesity and cellulite.

Recharge and Revive

Today, guests enjoy gently bubbling thermal waters in hotel pools across Dolenjske Toplice and at the town's highly rated **Wellness Center Balnea**. Here, vast pools of whirling, gushing, fizzing warm waters soothe, pummel and ease cares away in lagoons, grottos, waterfalls and tubs. Positive energy, holistic well-being, vitality and mental strength have become all-

3 things you **must not** miss

◀ 1 Trip to Soteska
Marvel at the architectural and historic sites in nearby Soteska, including the ruins of a once-mighty castle and a garden pavilion known as the Hudičev turn (Devil's Tower).
www.dolenjske-toplice.si

2 Historical Site in Forest
Explore the vine-tangled, dense forest region of Kočevski Rog and its tree-shrouded Baza 20 (Base 20), a settlement of barracks dating from 1943.
www.dolmuzej.com

3 Town Holiday
Revel in the festivities, dance, food and song of the town's lively municipal holiday on 22 July. Topliška noč is the loudest, biggest and most celebrated cultural event in the town's calendar.
www.dolenjske-toplice.si

important goals for spa-goers in Dolenjske Toplice, who not only seek the highest degree of relaxation and a major recharge of the batteries but also lifestyle tips and a wellness plan.

Carefully designed flower-trimmed parklands provide the perfect setting for restful recuperation relaxing solitude, with tree-shaded benches overlooking a backdrop of verdant hills – a powerful scenic antidote to the fast-paced tensions of the high-tech world. Hydrotherapy using warm-water tubs, indoor and outdoor thermal pools and a therapy pool promise to tantalize every sensory trigger in order to promote an enhanced feeling of well-being. Water temperature in the open-air pools is 27°C (81°F), with indoor pools at 32°C (90°F). Each has massaging jets (air and water) and other underwater massage nozzles.

In recent years, the Wellness Center Balnea has added a highly popular array of couples therapies comprising sensual whirlpool baths, a pampering perspiration massage, a scented massage for two and bathing.

At the well-equipped 102-room **Hotel Vital**, built in 1776, the thermal waters in the hotel pools form a sister facility to the Wellness Center Balnea. Offering its own range of sensual showers, powerful underwater massage and a wide variety of different touch therapies, from anti-cellulite treatments and head massages to shiatsu and hot-stones therapies, the Vital also hosts yoga and meditation in synergy with the natural energy of the garden surroundings where dozens of bird-filled walking trails lead up to lofty peaks and summits. One- and five-day programmes are also available.

INFORMATION

WELLNESS CENTER BALNEA
t +386 7 391 9750
w www.terme-krka.si

Pay €7.20 for use of the mineral-water pools or book an exquisite spa package, such as the couples programme at €149.

HOTEL VITAL
t +386 7 391 9441
w www.terme-krka.si

A three-hour or more session in the hotel's pools is from €10.

CROATIA

travel essentials

TIME ZONE: GMT +1

TELEPHONE CODE: +385

CURRENCY: Kuna

CAPITAL: Zagreb

LANGUAGE: Croatian

WHEN TO GO: The temperature in April and September is mild, in contrast summers can be oppressively hot but the days are long and sunny. By October the weather is cooler but still suitable for outdoor pursuits. In early November the cold sets in – as do the wind and rain.

Zadar

It may be thick, black, greasy and have a pungent stench, but the mud from the town of Nin, close to the city of Zadar in Croatia's northern Dalmatian region, is much revered.

Used in traditional, natural healing practices for many centuries, the gooey peloid gloop (called '*blato*' in Croatian) forms the largest curative mud deposits in the Adriatic. Found in areas of Nin's long, sandy, alluvial peninsula where shallow tides leave areas of the grass-fringed shoreline exposed, the curative sludge is gathered from boggy, low-lying terrain.

Moisture-rich Mud

Today, modern health tourism remains central to Zadar and the surrounding area, a region blessed with outstanding microclimatic conditions and clear, pure seawater. Even Londoners and Parisians have joined the hordes of Italians, Slovenians, Austrians and domestic health tourists on their annual fix of wellness therapy with programmes often priced according to the individual's wallet. Worry lines, stress and fatigue are soon replaced by contentment and calm amid the heady pong of sulphur after a morning of mud therapy, massage and a balmy seawater swim.

Mud Treatments

As you'd expect from a destination touting natural therapies, the style of mud application can be informal. Clothes are often optional (go bare if you dare as it'll spare your threads from the fetid gloop). At the **Hotel & Spa Iadera** a 2-cm (¾-in) thick layer of mud is applied directly on your skin using a wooden paddle. You're then wrapped in a kind of plastic before being rolled up in a succession of blankets in the style of an overstuffed sofa. As your body – and the coal-coloured viscous slathering – starts to heat up you'll begin to feel wonderfully warm and cosseted, if a little itchy. Soon you're a foul-smelling mess, steaming like a cowpat with the

ABOVE Detoxifying mud therapy at the Hotel & Spa Iadera.

OPPOSITE Church of St Donat, Zadar Old Town.

3 things you **must not** miss

1 Walk Along the Prom
Take a walk along the sea promenade Riva to breathe in pure coastal air, enjoy lush green parks and absorb views of the Zadar Channel out to sea-spray islands, bobbing boats and seabirds.
www.visitzadar.net

2 Barter Like the Locals
The City Market, one of the best in Dalmatia, is the place to go for tasty locally grown produce such as olive oil, brandy (*rakija*), dried figs, honey, almond and cheeses.
www.visitzadar.net

▶ **3 Watch the Sun Go Down**
Enjoy the soft crimson-amber glow of the famous Zadar sunset, the most beautiful in the world according to Alfred Hitchcock.

INFORMATION

· · · · · · · · · · · · · · ·

HOTEL & SPA IADERA
t +385 23 206 624
w www.falkensteiner.com

*Check for seasonal spa
offers such as two-night
Pure Wellness Breaks from
€190 including a traditional
Croatian massage, sauna,
whirlpool, relaxation therapy,
scalp massage and a 40-
minute wrap in local mud.*

BELOW *Sun-drenched sands
on Zadar's seafront.*

tingle of micro-organisms and soft-bodied invertebrates wriggling against your skin. Yet even when covered in decomposed dollops of gunk the therapeutic benefits are undeniable. First, the loamy sludge generates a stratospheric sweat that flushes the body of potentially harmful toxins. The therapeutic mud drives minerals deep into the body tissue where it is most needed, aided by the natural pressure of the mud pack's weightiness. It is not uncommon for your body heat to surge towards 40°C (104°F) before you are ceremoniously unwrapped. At this point you already feel lighter, brighter and cleaner – from the inside out. Sometimes you'll be showered off with a high-velocity cold-water hose. Kinder therapists will gently mop you down with a tepid cloth before insisting you take a swim in the sea.

While the therapy doesn't yield dramatic instant results, the healing continues for hours after the mud has been removed. You'll notice that your skin tone may have altered for the better, muscles will feel less fatigued, shoulders will be free from tension and constipated digestive tracts will unblock. You'll likely experience a glow of blissful happiness that runs all over you until you close your eyes and simply breathe for a while. There is something extremely satisfying about falling into bed utterly exhausted by a day of mud wrapping, rigorous massage and swimming – you'll feel like you'll live to reach a hundred even though you may never be able to wash the smell of sulphur out of your hair.

SERBIA

travel essentials

TIME DIFFERENCE: GMT +1

TELEPHONE CODE: +381

CURRENCY: Serbian dinar

CAPITAL: Belgrade

LANGUAGE: Serbian

WHEN TO GO: Serbia enjoys a typical Mediterranean climate of mild winters and hot, dry summers, with highest temperatures in the central provinces and the coolest regions in the highlands. The average mid-summer temperature is 24°C (75°F).

Brestovačka Banja

Benefiting from a temperate continental climate that lavishes the region with around 200 sunny days a year, Brestovačka Banja is renowned Serbia-wide for its natural curative powers.

ABOVE Lake Borsko Jezero.

RIGHT Interior of spa building.

OPPOSITE Pavilion in spa gardens.

PREVIOUS PAGE Ribarska Banja (see page 114).

Situated 400m (1,312ft) above sea level, Brestovačka Banja is nestled among 90ha (222 acres) of fragrant pine trees in the foothills of the Crni Vrh Mountain beside the tip of Lake Borsko Jezero, 280km (174 miles) south-east of Belgrade.

Precious Waters

The resort is home to 10 sources of thermo-mineral waters with a temperature range of 32–42°C (90–108°F). Rich in calcium, sodium, magnesium, iron oxides, aluminium, silicon, chlorine, iodine, bromine, phosphate, nitrate, zinc and fluoride – among others – Brestovačka Banja's waters have been hailed as a reputable healing force in the treatment of rheumatoid ailments since Roman and Byzantine times and during Turkish rule. After liberation from the Turks in 1833, the spa town became an important wellness centre in the Principality of Serbia. Princess Ljubica and her sons visited the spa town in

3 things you **must not** miss

◄ 1 Magnificent Caves
Delve into the Zlotske Caves – Lazareva and Vernjikica. Access allows upper-level exploration through 11 stalagmite-filled chambers and ravines of pure white calcite. Contact Bors tourist office. *t +381 30 24 166*

2 Hiking and Fishing
Take a hike out into forest that surrounds the resort or venture to the calm, fish-filled waters of Lake Borsko Jezero. Contact the local tourist information office for advice, maps, etc. *t +381 30 31 830*

3 Visit Grand Palace
Visit the Palace of Prince Aleksandar, Serbia's ruler between 1842 and 1858, and the old royal hunting grounds in a dominant, lofty position on steep terrain overlooking the town. *www.serbia.travel*

1834, prompting an immediate chemical analysis of the water and the construction of spa buildings in 1837. As a popular wellness destination with the royal household, Brestovačka Banja soon became the most frequented of Serbia's wellness resorts, earning considerable fame for its curative might. Therapies involved water consumption and treatments, including bathing, drinking, spraying, rinsing, and as an aid in medicaments.

Sunny, Sheltered and Spring-fed

Today, Brestovačka is synonymous with helping people to recover from physical and mental exhaustion. Several natural springs gurgle and surge along the banks of the Pujica River though only 10 of them have been chemically and balneologically tested. The town's communal baths were restored in 1968 and the original Turkish steam room in 1970. Treatments are carried out in adjoining therapy suites and can be booked through participating hotels.

Spa treatments include bathing, drinking, spraying, rinsing, showering and aerosol therapies that maximize the naturally healing effects of the waters against a backdrop of green forests in spring, golden fields in summer, red leaves in autumn and deep snow in winter. Wellness tourists can mountaineer, hike to the peaks with a picnic, and fish in Lake Borsko Jezero. Physical activities are designed to improve cardiovascular health, stamina and circulation and help to boost the nervous system. It is entirely up to you how much you want to exert yourself, and care is taken by the staff not to put joints and muscles under strain. All recreation activities are created with enjoyment in mind.

All of Brestovačka Banja's small, family-run hotels offer a spa-booking service. The **Hotel Dom Odmora** and the **Hotel Srpska Kruna** are two of the town's most popular places to stay with wellness tourists looking for cosy comfort in the centre of town, close to the mineral-water springs and pumps.

INFORMATION

HOTEL DOM ODMORA
t +381 30 439 622

Meaning 'House of Rest' this 1950s lodge benefits from spring-fed thermal waters and surrounding wildflower forests. Facilities include a sports centre and therapy suites offering massages from 2,400 RSD.

HOTEL SRPSKA KRUNA
t +381 30 477 078

This 175-room hotel is set in 100ha (247 acres) of woodlands. The hotel offers a full spa booking and referral service.

Ribarska Banja

A popular destination spa for post-operative recovery, Ribarska Banja is famous throughout Serbia for its beautiful surrounding woodlands, invigorating fresh air and naturally restorative ambience.

ABOVE Open-air bathing at Ribarska Banja.

OPPOSITE Villa Srbija, Ribarska Banja Spa.

In central Serbia, the pretty spa town of Ribarska Banja sits on the tree-clad side of Mount Jastrebac at 540m (1,772ft) above sea level. The town has six mineral-water springs (38–42°C (100–108°F)), which are often compared to the famous French Pyrenees mountain springs. With a centuries-old reputation for wellness, the town offers a variety of year-round well-being programmes that centre on remedying the symptoms of exhaustion, anxiety, long-term illness and frazzled nerves.

Rural Oasis

Set in thick, green, wooded folds of gorgeous countryside, Ribarska Banja is a pollution-free rural oasis blessed with fresh, pure air and a plenitude of thermo-mineral resources that have proven effective in the treatment of modern-day stress. Here, the term 'wellness' has long focused on achieving a healthy lifestyle through nutritious food, physical activity, relaxation and positive mental health. Visitors to Ribarska Banja will discover a wide range of therapies that are thought to be highly beneficial in improving psyche-physical health.

Complete Wellness Package

Ribarska Banja's most popular wellness therapies include hydromassages, whirlpool baths, sauna, steam room, inhalations and over 30 different styles of massage, from hot oil and herbal infusions to deep-tissue and lymphatic drainage. Physical fulfilment is encouraged via walks through the forest to babbling brooks and wildlife-filled clearings surrounded by aromatic wildflowers and shrubs. At the 510-room **Ribarska Banja Spa**, the focus is on holistic well-being coupled with clinical treatments. The accommodation comprises single and double rooms, and spacious, high-quality self-contained apartments within nine villas. Many of the apartments overlook the forested slopes of

3 things you **must not** miss

◀ 1 Nearby Monasteries
Take a trip to the splendid history-rich monasteries in the surrounding countryside, including St Roman and Pokrov Presvete Bogorodice in Djunis – both popular day-trip excursions. *www.ribarska banja.co.rs*

2 River Rafting
Rafting on the River Južna Morava is a popular activity with visitors to this spa town. *www.ribarskabanja.co.rs*

3 Cultural Events
The town has a busy cultural and artistic calendar, with regular theatre performances, plays, folklore shows, music festivals, art exhibitions, food festivals and handicraft exhibitions. *www.ribarska banja.co.rs*

INFORMATION

· · · · · · · · · · · · · · · · · · ·

RIBARSKA BANJA SPA

t +381 37 865 270
w www.ribarskabanja.co.rs

This 510-room wellness hotel offers a range of therapies to enhance physical and mental health. Popular detoxification and weight-loss programmes combine with bathing, whirlpools and massage, with treatments from 3,000 RSD.

Veliki Jastrebac Mountain, a sheltering shield that protects the town from cold winds and rapid temperature variations. This magical therapeutic combination of fresh air, a steady climate and homoeothermic and hypothermal waters ensures Ribarska Banja has been home to a health resort since the time of Turkish rule – at least.

Today, tourists are welcomed by newly refurbished wellness centres that may not be plush but are clean, comfortable and well equipped. The centre's signature detoxification programme that is said to help rid the body of excess toxins involves an aqua-detox pampering session, firm-pressure water massage, prescribed sauna usage, cleansing and restorative moisturizing. There is a menu of treatments using the thermo-mineral waters from the town's springs. Carefully prepared meals offer a balanced nutritional intake.

MONTENEGRO

travel essentials

TIME ZONE: GMT +1

TELEPHONE CODE: +382

CURRENCY: Euro

CAPITAL: Podgorica

LANGUAGE: Serbian

WHEN TO GO: Hot, dry summers and mild, wet winters characterize Montenegro's Mediterranean coastal climate. In the central plains, temperatures can hit the upper 30°Cs (100°F+), with typical mid-summer temperatures averaging 25°C (77°F). Highland regions are cooler, with snowfall throughout the winter months.

Herceg Novi

Herceg Novi's wellness industry began in earnest in early 1929, when the town's age-old claims regarding its healing sea mud (*igaljsko blato*) received official government endorsement.

Soon international recognition ensued, not just for the mud but also for the mineral-water springs (*igaljske slatine*). The town has become renowned throughout Montenegro as the birthplace of healthcare and wellness tourism. Wedged between the highest mountain of the Dinara Massif, Orjen at 1,895m (6,217ft), and the mouth of the beautiful Bay of Kotor (Boka Kotorska) on the Adriatic, Herceg Novi is characterized by bountiful lush greenery and over 250 sunny days a year. Warm, crystal-clear sparkling seas offer a long swimming season with water temperatures between 22° and 26°C (72° and 79°F).

Institute Igalo

Herceg Novi is home to the prestigious Institute Igalo, the largest spa and health centre in the Mediterranean. The institute is a stalwart promoter of thalassotherapy, mud cures and the powers of preventative medicine. Tailored programmes offer each guest a spa prescription that allows a unique focus on individual health and wellness goals. Many choose to immerse themselves in the tactile therapies of the spa's massage suite while for others the allure of hydration therapies and facials using nourishing mineral-rich waters are impossible to resist. Organic mud body packs are a popular traditional Herceg Novi speciality, as is taking a dip in the thermal pool – one of the town's most simple relaxing and rejuvenating pleasures.

Preventative philosophies are impressive at the Institute Igalo, where a diverse array of therapies and programmes is dedicated to helping the body fight illness and avert stress, tension, aches and pains. High-grade professional spa and health practitioners take time to introduce the wellness benefits of their soothing aquatic world. A mineral-laden salt-rich composition

ABOVE *Herceg Novi coastline.*

OPPOSITE *Herceg Novi.*

3 things you **must not** miss

1 Old Town Walk
Walk the historic Old Town with its unique architectural centre to marvel at the fine landmark structures. *www.montenegro.com/city/herceg_novi*

2 Town Garden
Breathe in the aromatic plants and admire the exotic blooms and towering shrubs in the botanic garden in the very heart of the town, which was formerly the park of the Hotel Boka. *www.hercegnovi.cc*

▶ 3 Island Boat Trip
Take a boat out to uninhabited Mamula Island (also called Lastavica Island), at the entrance to the stunning Bay of Kotor, to enjoy dense, lush vegetation and a charming beach on this popular summer day trip. *www.hercegnovi.cc*

INFORMATION

· · · · · · · · · · · · · · · · ·

INSTITUTE IGALO

t +382 31 658 111
w www.igalospa.com

*Choose from medical,
physiotherapy, beauty or
wellness therapy menus.
Curative detoxifying
mudbaths and wraps from
€15 and to-die-for
massages using sea-flower
oils from €24.*

characterizes the local waters while the healing, mildly radioactive mud (peloid) gathered from Topljanski Bay is a mix of bioactive sedimentation of mineral alluviums, sand and decaying sea flora and fauna.

Believing that a healthy diet is paramount to good health and well-being, the Institute Igalo serves simple, fresh, locally grown food. Prepared by a team of chefs in conjunction with advice from doctors, nutritionists and dieticians, an ever-changing culinary menu features plenty of fresh seafood, lamb, veal and chicken as well as low-fat and low-sugar cake and ice cream.

Independent Travel

Of course, you don't need to frequent the Institute Igalo to absorb the wellness traditions, diet ethos and curative therapies of Herceg Novi. Independent travellers can stay in a hotel and follow the locals down to the muddy sand, swim in the mildly radioactive mineral-rich waters and eat at the small family-run establishments around the promenade, where fresh, local seafood is served

(ignore all of the greasy fast-food outlets). To stretch the limbs, work the cardiovascular system and get the blood pumping, take one of the scenic, ancient stone paths that wind up the hillside out of town to some of the outlying rural villages. Many of the paths link up and offer a picturesque 6.5-km (4-mile) uphill stomp, complete with stunning panoramic views. This will give your quadriceps and gluteus maximus muscles a workout for free.

*ABOVE RIGHT View of
Herceg Novi.*

*RIGHT Exercise class at
Institute Igalo.*

Ulcinj

As the southernmost city of the Montenegrin coast, Ulcinj is blessed by geology and geography that have furnished it with an exceptional array of natural good fortunes.

ABOVE Lake Skadar.

Renowned for its clear, sparkling water (visibility reaches 38m (125ft) in summer), ultra-fine sandy beaches and year-round warm, sunny climate, Ulcinj is also home to sulphur-rich curative waters, medicinal mud, sea salt and coastal ions. Associated with good health for several centuries, Ulcinj is much more than a seaside sanatorium, it is a place that is now ingrained in the Montenegrin psyche for its wellness benefits. Proclaimed a 'spa and climatic resort' in 1922 by a decree of the Kingdom of Yugoslavia on account of its bath-like warm seas (May–October), Ulcinj has around 2,700 hours of sunshine per year (around 7.4 hours a day on average).

Today, health tourists continue to walk barefoot across Ulcinj's outstandingly pure, fine sands, a velvety carpet free from traces of soil, mud or organic matter. Comprised of some 30 biological minerals and characterized by low levels of radioactivity,

the sand is used in spa therapies as an aid to suppleness, to boost energy and improve mobility.

Ladies Beach

All this is just a stone's throw from therapeutic sulphur springs that surge up next to the sea close to the sands of Zenska Plaža ('Ladies Beach'), where thousands of women have sought Mother Nature's Montenegrin cure for infertility. The history of Zenska Plaža is cloaked in magical fairytales, myths and legends based on the medicinal qualities of the waters – the nutrient-rich prehistoric mud (peloid) and the sea salt harvested from the Ulcinj salt works. In ancient times, Muslim women sought a cure for sterility in these springs – a practice believed to be the origin of Ladies Beach and its role in aiding fertility.

According to scientific examinations, the local mud possesses high-grade

3 things you **must not** miss

1 Seaplane Sightseeing

Enjoy a seaplane flight over Lake Skadar, a sparkling body of water rich in wildlife, flora, birds and cultural and historic monuments spread across wetlands, woodlands and hilly plains. *www.visit-montenegro.com/skadar-lake.htm*

2 Amazon of Montenegro

Delve into the basin region dubbed the 'Amazon of Montenegro' around the mighty Bojana River. The Bojana is famed for its diverse array of flora and fauna and the paradise isle of Ada sat right in its mouth. *www.ulcinj365.com*

▶ **3 River Adventure**

Go white-water rafting on the UNESCO-protected Tara River Gorge, the deepest canyon in Europe at 1,300m (4,265ft). Its 78-km (48½-mile) route passes waterfalls, bridges, Roman roads and rugged countryside. *www.visit-ulcinj.com*

mineral qualities that rank it among the best discovered on the Adriatic to date. Ulcinj's saline basin and oxygen-rich pine forests provide the ideal setting for women contemplating motherhood – you'll see many strolling along the sea shore where the purest, freshest coastal air can be imbibed. The pine forest canopy is believed to be enriched with natural resin aroma – another positive curative power. Ladies Beach offers curious waters composed of a mix of sulphur from underwater springs, radium and sea salts. Although the therapeutic springs may not be widely known outside of Montenegro, the water sources in the Albatros and Valdanos springs are packed with minerals reputed to be a curative blend for oviduct conditions.

Swimming in the waters isn't enough to become pregnant, with local lore insisting there is a ritual to be respected. The would-be mother, accompanied by an older local woman, should visit a sulphur-rich cave that the locals call 'the cave with a bad smell'. After undressing, the would-be mother should walk several times around a stone immersed in sulphurous brown water in the middle of the cave. Once this ritual has been completed, she then needs to consume a boiled egg brought for this purpose. Rumour has it, once a woman has conceived she can also influence the baby's gender by the way she washes herself in the flow.

Nature's Bounty

Exploited for its therapeutic qualities and wellness potential since time immemorial, Ulcinj has the longest beach on the Adriatic coast (Velika Plaža at 13km (8 miles) stretching out from Djerane Cape) together with a clothes-optional river island blessed with paradisiacal sands, Ada Bojana – the perfect place to commune with nature au naturel. Located in the marginal subtropical zone of the European Mediterranean, Ulcinj covers an area of 255sq km (98½sq miles), on which olives, figs, citrus fruits, almonds, kiwi fruits, chestnuts, pomegranates, grapevines, cereal crops, pears, apples and plums thrive. A staggering variety of river, lake and sea fish together with authentic local brandy and wines make the Ulcinj table fresh, wholesome and distinctive.

Nearby Nacionalni park Skadarsko jezero (Lake Skadar National Park) has long been a setting for peaceful meditation. The 44-km (27½-mile) lake straddles Montenegro and Albania. One of the largest bird reserves in Europe, the park is home to 270 bird species, among them the last pelicans in Europe. Containing small islands covered by wild pomegranate, laurel and tangled ivy, Lake Skadar is popular with outdoor yoga practitioners and meditation groups who seek waterside quietude among the avian-filled foliage.

Accommodation Option

One of the town's most notable health complexes is the wellness centre at the **Hotel Imperial**, where a state-of-the-art therapeutic facility offers a comprehensive well-being programme using a mix of local natural cures and expert medical care. Opt for mud wraps, marine therapies, a range of clinical treatments or holistic health programmes run by a team that embrace alternative healing concepts alongside conventional medicine.

ABOVE *View of Ulcinj's old town.*

OPPOSITE *Pure, fine, curative sands of Ulcinj beach.*

ROMANIA

travel essentials

TIME DIFFERENCE: **GMT +2**

TELEPHONE CODE: **+40**

CURRENCY: **Leu**

CAPITAL: **Bucharest**

LANGUAGE: **Romanian**

WHEN TO GO: Scorching summer highs form a sharp contrast with cold snowy winters. June, July and August are hottest near the Black Sea coast, where average temperatures reach 24–30°C (75–86°F). In summer there are frequent showers and thunderstorms in the mountains. Pleasant autumn days keep the sunshine going until mid-October, but Transylvania and the Carpathian Mountains can be wet year-round.

Băile Herculane

Located in the country's scenic south-west, Băile Herculane (Hercules Spa) is one of Romania's most fabled wellness resorts. It is the nation's oldest and one of the world's most ancient spa centres.

With an attestation dating back to the year AD 153, the resort area was developed during the early 1700s under Austrian rule. Grand edifices in impressive Austrian baroque style graced the resort and the spa drew affluent visitors through its therapeutic virtues and healing thermo-mineral waters. Roman emperor Marcus Aurelius, with his mother Julia, bathed here a number of times, while Austrian emperor Franz Joseph visited in 1852, declaring Băile Herculane 'the most beautiful resort in Europe'.

Mineral Waters and Fresh Air

Drenching in the spa's mineral waters allows small traces of a curative mix to permeate the skin amid air packed with beneficial negative ions – a wellness concoction that is particularly restful, relaxing and restorative. Set on the banks of the Cerna River, in a low-lying corridor separating the Godeanu Mountains and the Cernei Mountains from the Valcanului and Mehedinti peaks, Băile Herculane boasts the fresh, lofty air of an alpine retreat despite being at an altitude of just 168m (551ft). Benefiting from the unspoilt splendour of the 60,000-ha (148,263-acre) Parcul Naţional Domogled-Valea Cernei (Domogled-Cerna Valley National Park) and its thick forests of beech and pine trees, Băile Herculane is rich in wild herbs, flowers and shrubs that are used in traditional wellness practices. Health ideals stem from a proud folkloric tradition centred on the countryside in a region recognized for its considerable ethnographical value.

With over 16 springs tapped thus far, a free-flowing supply of thermal mineral waters have their source along a 4-km (2½-mile) stretch of the leafy River Cerna. Of these, the main springs of Neptun, Diana,

ABOVE Statue of Hercules in central square.

OPPOSITE Quaint town of Mediaş (see page 126).

3 things you must not miss

1 Cave of Thieves
Visit the impressive three-chambered Peştera Hotilor (Cave of Thieves), situated on a rocky side of a sheer cliff overlooking the fast-running Cerna River. Ask at the local tourist information office for details of how to get there.

2 Explore the Resort
Take a 2–3-hour stroll around local attractions on a route that starts at Hercules Square, past the Hotel Roman to the Cerna Waterfall, to a popular swimming spot fed by mineral-rich springs. Pick up a map from any local hotel.

▶ 3 Nature Walks
Enjoy nature walks in the scenic Semenic Mountains and Cerna Valley among wildlife-rich (voles, shrews, bears and deer) fragrant forests, meadows and rugged peaks. The local tourist information office will provide routes and maps.

Hebe, Apollo 1, Iosif, Hercules and Hygeea feed the majority of spa buildings, aided by hydro-drilling projects that boost the flow of water. Bathing therapies at Băile Herculane exploit the curative properties of these radiation-laden waters packed with chlorine and sodium. In 1970, the Parc Vicol was unveiled as Băile Herculane's striking centrepiece, an oasis of trees, blooms and fountains that draws spa-goers to this day.

Bed and Bathing

At the chichi **Vila Hera,** a gorgeous outdoor thermo-sulphurous water pool is used for the treatment of aches and pains, and is believed to be particularly effective for the back and hips and for menstrual cramps. Guests can also book a range of spa procedures, from luxuriant full-body massages and reflexology to anti-ageing facial wraps. The place is

family owned and run by friendly staff that will organize hikes, activities and leisure trips – as well as therapies in sister spas.

Though simple and fairly basic, the popular **Hotel Roman** offers excellent value for money if frills aren't your thing. First-rate amenities include around 150 rooms, a restaurant, terrace, bar and hairdressing salon together with swimming pool, sauna and gym. Underground, in the old basement space, the remnants of the imperial Roman baths can be found – now the town's Terma Romana (Roman Bath Museum).

The modern 270-room **Hercules Hotel** is characterized by new, contemporary-styled rooms and a slew of clinical-looking therapy suites. Located right on the Cerna River, the spa specializes in hydrotherapy, electrotherapy, rehabilitation, physiotherapy and acupuncture.

INFORMATION

. . . .

VILA HERA

t + 40 722 756 247

w www.vilahera.ro

Highly recommended reflexology and deep-tissue massage therapies in the spa suite are priced from 85 RON.

HOTEL ROMAN

t +40 255 560 390

Relax in the pool or sauna, work out in the gym or visit the remnants of the town's imperial Roman baths, located in the basement. Use the thermal suite (pool, sauna and massage) from 90 RON.

HERCULES HOTEL

t +40 255 560 880

Medical in atmosphere with therapists in starched white aprons, tiled therapy suites and bright neon strip lights, this much-acclaimed spa hotel has a sterling reputation for acupuncture, hot- and cold-mineral-water treatments, massage and mud wraps from 95 RON.

LEFT *The Latin inscription on the building housing the resort's springs translates as: Holy Water of Hercules.*

OPPOSITE *The fine, domed spa pavilion is a central landmark.*

Bazna

Enjoying considerable scenic splendour, the spa town of Bazna sits in the heart of Transylvania in central Romania's Sibiu County, amid deep forests, gushing streams and charming medieval settlements.

ABOVE Touch therapies are central to wellness treatments.

OPPOSITE Salt-rich pool in the renovated Ocna Sibiului Spa.

Established in 1302 by early settlers, Bazna became a full-fledged wellness resort in 1842 on account of its plentiful natural healing riches – therapeutic mud, mineral waters and salts rich in iodine and bromine. Earning great curative acclaim for its success in treating a variety of ear, nose and throat conditions, stress-related conditions, rheumatoid disorders and a plenitude of general well-being concerns, Bazna's well-being centres extol the benefits of frequent bathing in thermal pools, massages using organic mud and salt grains, mud packs and saltwater steam treatments. Served by Sibiu and Târgu Mureş airports, Bazna is also accessible from Bucharest by train via Mediaş and Târnăveni, ensuring a steady flow of domestic wellness tourists from the capital as well as international travellers.

Natural Resources
Characterized by slow flowing waters of 0.33 litres (½pt) per second, Bazna's cool (13°C (55°F)), healing waters are sodic and hypertonic with traces of bromide. Boasting a pliable, soft plasticity and fine dispersion, the local mud is rich in decaying plant matter. Average air temperatures of 8.6°C (47.5°F) are praised as a natural sedative – ideal for convalescing visitors seeking good-quality, restorative sleep.

Almost conjoined with sister town Ocna Sibiului, Bazna benefits from the region's flooded ancient salt mines. Today, these salt-rich water masses form the basis of a sizeable menu of naturopathic therapies, from saline bathing to ease rheumatic, dermatological, endocrine and gynaecological complaints to whirlpool, sauna and steam cures for respiratory illnesses.

Spa Options
The mid-range **Hotel Expro** in Bazna, a modern spa centre (open since 2000), centres on a saltwater pool with an array of

3 things you **must not** miss

◄ 1 Bazna's Gothic Church
Bazna's Gothic church dates back to 1302 and was built by Transylvanian Saxons. It now has Romanesque architectural features as well as ornate touches from the 15th and 16th centuries.

2 Day Trip to Mediaş
Stroll the quaint cobbled streets of the medieval town of Mediaş (16km (10 miles) south-east of Bazna), a traditional, strongly fortified, Transylvanian settlement.
www.romaniatourism.com/ medias.html

3 Local Wine Producer
Enjoy the striking vine-terraced scenery of the Tarnave Vineyard and Jidvei Winery (24km (15 miles) west of Bazna), one of Romania's major white-wine producers.
www.jidvei.ro

INFORMATION

∙ ∙ ∙ ∙ ∙ ∙ ∙ ∙ ∙ ∙ ∙ ∙ ∙ ∙ ∙ ∙ ∙ ∙

HOTEL EXPRO

t +40 269 831 512

w www.bazna.ro

In-house mineral pools are free for guests' use and other on-site recreational facilities include tennis courts. Budget for 150 RON for mud wraps and facials.

OCNA SIBIULUI SPA

t +40 269 577 387

w www.ocnasibiului.ro

An ever-changing treatment menu offers medical procedures and therapies à la carte, from around 120 RON. Use of pools (indoor and outdoor) free.

HOTEL SALINAS

t +40 269 577 387

w www.ocnasibiului.ro

Expect to pay around 140 RON for a 40-minute full-body massage using herb-infused oils.

all-natural Bazna salt cures. A menu of organic wraps, baths and massages use mineral waters and native herbs. Leisure activities are also offered including country hikes to unique villages rich in Transylvanian folklore and bracing walks to many of the region's stunning natural attractions.

Nearby, the **Ocna Sibiului Spa** has been wholly renovated in order to restore the original Viennese architects' design to its former glory. With a new central pavilion and beautifully upgraded facades, the spa enjoys the peaceful tranquillity of a leafy location. With a dizzying array of salt-deposit therapies, the spa also has a mineral-water pool and a slew of functional, modern therapy suites that offer deep-tissue massage, balneotherapy and thermotherapy (mud and paraffin treatments).

One of the accommodation options for those wanting to visit the Ocna Sibiului Spa is the **Hotel Salinas**. Although the rooms are simply furnished, the hotel does have an impressive sauna, massage suites and a team of visiting spa therapists. Don't expect deep-pile fluffy dressing gowns and fruit baskets at this bed-and-board budget option but the location is right in the heart of town close to restaurants, bars and the main spa attractions.

Eforie Nord

Eforie Nord is renowned for its blessed coastal climate. The weather remains mild throughout the winter months, earning it a long-heralded reputation for seaside cures.

ABOVE Treatment at the Ana Aslan Health Spa.

OPPOSITE Seafront at Constanţa.

During the 1950s, the town was dubbed 'the St Tropez of the East', with its quiet, narrow backstreets packed with coastal charm, yacht-moored promenade and stunning sea views. Over 3km (2 miles) of golden sandy beaches characterize Eforie Nord's scenic shoreline, interspersed with half a dozen rocky breakwaters and lined with seaside bars and restaurants.

Famous Waters

The seawater here is famous throughout Romania for its high sodium content, while the lakes boast a mildly mineralized composition, so Eforie Nord offers natural-health fans a myriad of bathing options. High concentrates of saline are used in aerosol therapies, steam treatments and salty underwater massages, with the waters from Lake Techirghiol – a major curative source – five times brinier than the sea. When a cool wind blows, white stripes appear on the surface of the waters of the lake, such is its high salinity. According to local legend, a crippled and blind old man, riding on a donkey, rode close to the lake by mistake and got stuck in the smelly mud along its shores. After struggling to get free for hours, the man realized that a mysterious force was drawing the donkey towards the lake. Miraculously he could then see a bright light shining over the surface of the lake and he noticed that the bad wounds on his donkey's head had healed and that his old body was youthful. He told the local people about this, prompting a rush to the shores to bath and wallow in the mud. Miracles are said to have happened here with seriously ill people being restored to full health.

Today, numerous therapeutic packs and wraps use the biologically active sediment from the bottom of lake – a nutrient-laden cure known locally as *namol*, which is black, dense, stinky and extraordinarily coarse. Medical

3 things you **must not** miss

◀ 1 Day Trip to Constanţa
Visit the National History and Archaeology Museum or simply stroll around the streets to see the Roman walls and the longest mosaic pavements in the world. *www.romaniatourism.com/ constanta.html*

2 Europa Yacht Club
One of the best and most exclusive private beaches in town, with perfectly manicured sands, a swanky bar and fine restaurant. *www.anahotels.ro*

3 Cliffs and Headlands
Explore the soaring cliffs, flanked by a seafront promenade lined with cafes, bars and restaurants. Several walks link Eforie's northern and southern beaches via windswept scenic headlands.

experts testify that it is highly beneficial to sufferers of rheumatism, arthritis and gynaecological ailments.

Therapies and Treatments

In spas throughout Eforie Nord you can enjoy a range of dipping and swimming choices in a selection of indoor and outdoor pools filled with water brought from the lake. Or you can choose seawater bathing amid bird-filled marshes and oak forests rich in medicinal plant life.

Guests at the **Ana Aslan Health Spa** should be prepared to be overwhelmed by the sheer choice of therapies on offer, with over 16 specialized facial treatments alone. Full-day pampering packages include thermal dips, sauna, steam room and mineral-water showers together with a choice of de luxe massage and facial treatments – each one alluring, decadent and inviting.

Although the **Hotel Azur** doesn't offer therapies, it is partnered with the all-natural **Grand Clinique Centre**, where a vast therapy menu focuses on organic herbal therapies, indigenous plants, applications of local mud and the healing properties of the town's thermal and mineral baths.

Guests that stay at the Hotel Azur can also pre-book appointments at the highly respected **Steaua de Mare Hospital**, which offers a wide range of balneological treatments for mobility problems, bodily stresses and strains, circulatory ailments and metabolic illnesses.

INFORMATION

ANA ASLAN HEALTH SPA, HOTEL EUROPA
t +40 241 702 818
w www.anahotels.ro

An impressive spa menu features year-round full-day pampering programmes that start at just 300 RON – superb value for top-notch therapies in luxurious surroundings.

HOTEL AZUR
t +40 241 741 675
w www.hotelazur.ro

Conveniently located for spa and beach access, this modern hotel is partnered with the Grand Clinique Centre and the Steaua de Mare Hospital.

BULGARIA

travel essentials

TIME ZONE: GMT +2

TELEPHONE CODE: +359

CURRENCY: Lev

CAPITAL: Sofia

LANGUAGE: Bulgarian

WHEN TO GO: Northern Bulgaria has a moderate continental climate, while southern Bulgaria is distinctly Mediterranean. Summers are hot, winters are cool and crisp, while spring and autumn can be pleasantly mild. Half a dozen mountain ranges play a significant part in determining regional variances.

Hissarya

The town of Hissarya is one of Bulgaria's main spa destinations. It is a settlement that is synonymous with healthy living in the hearts and minds of Bulgarians.

During Roman rule, the town was a popular bathing centre with the moneyed elite and was blessed with grand emperor's palaces, wide stone streets, marble baths and numerous statues. Though largely destroyed by fires, Hissarya has retained remnants of its ancient walls together with some of the best-preserved fortress defences in Bulgaria.

Although the terrain is old, the wellness facilities in the town are ultra-modern and yet they are powered by over 20 natural mineral springs dating back thousands of years.

Water-based Therapies

Located on the outskirts of the Sredna Gora mountain range, close to the famous Valley of Roses, Hissarya is 167km (104 miles) east of Sofia. Bulgarians in need of fresh air, clean living, natural food and relaxation consider Hissarya the ultimate destination. The wellness therapies are focused on the local lightly mineralized waters. With a flow of about 4,000 litres (880 gallons) per minute, this healing elixir surges out of the ground at temperatures of between 27° and 51°C (81° and 124°F). The waters are belived to be particularly beneficial to patients with kidney, liver, pancreatic, digestive and gall bladder disorders.

Visitors can stroll through Hissarya taking nourishment from mineral-water drinking fountains and enjoying the leafy parklands of the Maiden Bath (Momina Banya) and its famous radioactive alkaline springs.

Spa Options

Every spa in Hissarya offers a comprehensive therapy programme using the town's waters. At the impressively equipped **Augusta Spa,** their balneology centre ranks among Bulgaria's finest.

ABOVE Mineral-water fountain.

OPPOSITE Beach near Varna (see page 136).

3 things you **must not** miss

1 Day at the Beach
Enjoy a swim at Hissarya's picturesque thermal-water beach, a popular family picnic venue and gathering place at weekends. *www.pd. government.bg*

2 Mountain Hike
Head to the outlying Sredna Gora mountain range for a hiking excursion across rugged, jutting peaks and loose-stone trails. *www.bg mountains.org*

▶ **3 Historic Walk**
Take a walk around the town's fortifications – the largest and best-preserved in Bulgaria. *www.plovdivguide.com*

AUGUSTA SPA HOTEL

t +359 337 62244

w www.augustaspa.com

Highly professional staff run a prestigious programme of curative water-based therapies. Delectable underwater body massages are priced from 97 lev.

SPA HOTEL HISSAR

t +359 337 62768

w www.hotelhissar.com

Sweet-smelling essential oils and herb-infused emulsions fill the air at this de luxe spa complex where standard massages start at 88 lev and sumptuous packages at 176 lev.

ASTRAEA SPA HOTEL

t +359 337 62211

w http://hotel-astraea.com

Asian and western European concepts combine with Eastern European health traditions at this spa. Exquisite massage packages from 107 lev.

The high-tech **Spa Hotel Hissar**'s much-acclaimed 'Fountain of Life' five- or seven-day programme centres on a tailored hydromassage using healing herbal aromas, curative colours and music to restore energy imbalances, with a to-die-for stress-busting massage as a relaxing finale.

Mixing a traditional health ethos with new-world spa ingredients, the **Astraea Spa Hotel** offers a delectable 50-minute Spring Fragrance body treatment using fresh produce with astringent properties and light, aromatic essential oils.

RIGHT Fountain in the centre of town.

Velingrad

As a hotbed of folkloric health traditions, Bulgaria boasts a lengthy heritage of naturopathic therapies. Herbal and floral essences from the fertile terrain feature heavily in Velingrad's thermal spa resorts.

Velingrad is situated at the western end of the Chepino Valley, where an abundance of mineral springs reach temperatures of up to 91°C (196°F). Another natural phenomenon is the Kleptuza – Bulgaria's biggest karst spring with an average flow of a staggering 1,200 litres (263 gallons) of ice-cold water per second.

St Spas' Day

At Chepino, the fabled St Spas site is adjacent to a prolific mineral spring. Each year, on the Thursday 40 days after Easter, joyous celebrations to honour the Saint of Spas on Spasovden (St Spas' Day) get underway with springtime gusto. Large crowds gather to celebrate life, love and good health.

This festival for the eternal human wish for health and joy is preceeded by Nymphs' Wednesday, when younger members of the community forage in the forests for the sweet-scented Burning Bush (*Dictamnus albus*), the red-blossomed flower of the elves and fairies. Used in naturopathy as a cure in its powdered root form and in delicate infusions, the therapeutic qualities of this aromatic floral herb are believed to ease fever, reduce inflammation and soothe colicky pains. On the eve of St Spas' Day, those suffering from illness sleep overnight in the woods where the Burning Bush grows in the belief they will awaken fully cured. According to legend, they should roll in dewy grass before yielding to slumber and trusting St Spas, who is considered the healer of all things living using the serenity and ecological medicines of the natural world.

Should it rain on Spasovden, the rain is considered to be golden because of the riches it brings to the grasses, plants, trees, crops, meadows and mineral-rich subterranean wells.

ABOVE Natural karst spring of Kleptuza.

3 things you **must not** miss

1 Skiing
In winter, ski the snow-heavy trails that characterize the scenic western end of the Chepino Valley, one of the most attractive areas of the majestic Rhodope Mountains. *www.pz.government.bg*

2 Archaeological Sites
Explore the numerous archaeological sites that scatter the landscape where rich findings, such as stone and bone tools and bronze artefacts have been left by Thracians, Slavs, Byzantines, and Romans.

▶ 3 Summer Boat Trip
In summer, take a boat out on beautiful Kleptuza Lake in Velingrad.

INFORMATION

SPA HOTEL DVORETSA

t +359 359 56 200

w www.dvoretsa.com

Though friendly staff speak just a smattering of English, expect them to tell you all about special 2-for-1 massage deals and discount therapy packages with a herbal oil massage just 68 lev for 70 blissful minutes.

GRAND HOTEL VELINGRAD

t + 359 884 770387

w www.grandhotel velingrad.com

Enjoy unhurried massage baths, mineral-water steam rooms, saunas and a host of body therapies using plants, spices, herbs, honey, milk and oils. Two-night stays are from 391 lev per person.

HOTEL ELBRUS

t + 359 53 239

w www.hotelelbrus.com

Offering great value for money (at packages from 195 lev per day), this modern wellness centre offers herbal health therapies, massage and a host of bathing rituals.

ABOVE One of the many fountains in the centre of town.

RIGHT Spa Hotel Dvoretsa is renowned for its hot- and cold-water healing treatments.

Spa Options

Visitors to Velingrad will discover an impressive range of facilities wholly dedicated to well-being, with the **Spa Hotel Dvoretsa** a particular highlight. Alongside a full range of hot- and cold-water hydrotherapy treatments you'll find a menu of around 30 different kinds of massages that draw exotic influences from all over world while remaining true to the Bulgarian health tradition. Some focus on relaxing and refreshing, others on skin hydration and improving the immune defence system, while many aim to balance energy, improve emotional well-being and cleanse and tone. While applying natural plant extracts, honey and mineral waters, a team of super-efficient therapists counsel spa-goers on all aspects of the importance of purification, stress reduction, detoxification and feeling good. It is easy to relax in suites that make full use of light, natural wood, exposed stone and earth tones in a spa hotel that has bountiful gardens, pine forests, tennis courts, shaded terraces and truly gorgeous countryside views.

Other fine wellness establishments include the highly regarded **Grand Hotel Velingrad** with its high-tech spa and the **Hotel Elbrus**, where rebalancing wellness programmes centre on spring-fed traditional bathing rituals.

Black Sea Coast

On Bulgaria's celebrated Black Sea Coast the healing benefits of organic springs and a coastal climate combine to offer beach-loving holidaymakers a highly popular therapeutic getaway.

Sea air, warm weather and negative air ionization all offer consider health benefits to wellness tourists in a region formed around 130km (81 miles) of white and golden sands. Drawing millions of visitors during the summer season (May–October), the Bulgarian Riviera (as it's been known since the fall of the Iron Curtain in 1989) is on an inland sea bounded by south-eastern Europe, the Caucasus and the Anatolian peninsula. It is renowned for its calm, languid waters, which ultimately are connected to the Atlantic Ocean via the Mediterranean and Aegean seas and various straits. Mineral springs and healing mud can be found across the region, with St Konstantin, Varna and Pomorie the oldest spa resorts.

Pomorie

In Pomorie, a seaside town on a narrow rocky peninsula on Burgas Bay, therapies at the **Grand Hotel Pomorie** are fed by a brackish lake revered as sacred by the ancient Thracians due to its curative properties. This stylish, modern wellness complex is situated close to the saline waters, ensuring a constant year-round supply. Therapies blend a modern spa menu with traditional Bulgarian balneotherapy complete with hydromassage tubs illuminated by 'mood lighting'.

Pomorie's location – blessed with low-lying seashore basins and iron-rich coastal sands – is much hailed for its favourable medicinal properties and these natural elements are used in a wide range of therapies along this curvy shoreline stretch. Medicinal sea baths take place in the smooth-bottomed shallows while Pomorie Lake provides great conditions for mud treatments. The mud deposits are notable for their fine structure, with an upper black layer with grey layers of clay-rich organic sludge

ABOVE Relax and enjoy the view at the Grand Hotel Pomorie.

3 things you **must not** miss

1 A Walk in Pomorie
Stroll in the historic centre of Pomorie, along pretty cobblestone streets that lead to the Preobrazhenie Gospodne Church, dating from 1765. *www. pomorie.com*

2 Shopping Trip
Shop till you drop in the bustling five-storey Sun City Centre in Burgas, where numerous clothes stores, boutiques, restaurants and chain stores vie for your attention. *www.suncity centre.com*

▶ 3 Varna's Scenic Spots
Revel in Varna's outlying quieter scenic spots along the coast, including the nature reserve of Kamchiya, the royal palace of Balchik and the hillside monastery of Aladzha. *www.varna.bg*

INFORMATION

GRAND HOTEL POMORIE
t +359 596 288 88
w www.grandhotel
    pomorie.com

Choose from a range of black-mud therapies, from gloopy wraps to peaty packs, priced from 68 lev.

ST GEORGE SPA HOTEL
t +359 596 244 11
w www.st-george-bg.info

Enjoy the relaxing pummelling effect of the mineral-water whirlpool tubs, free for guests' use. Double rooms cost from 59 lev per night and mud-wrap therapies are available from 39 lev.

APHRODITE BEAUTY SPA AND HEALTH CLINIC, HELIOS SPA & RESORT
t +359 52 356 108
w www.helios-spa.com

A huge menu of natural therapies offers plenty of choice – from saltwater scrubs and marine-rich facials to rich-oil body massages, from 107 lev.

ROMANCE SPA, ROMANCE SPLENDID HOTEL
t +359 52 385 400
w www.planexhotels.com

For the ultimate splurge, opt for a VIP suite priced from 254 lev, with the use of mineral-water pools included in the price.

ABOVE *Varna beach.*

underneath. Both are highly mineralized and packed with ancient plant sediment.

At the **St George Spa Hotel** in the heart of Pomerie's Old Quarter, sea views abound from a fine sun terrace. Delight in an outdoor whirlpool, relax in the indoor pool with a hydromassage suite or relish a warming mud therapy – just yards from the beach.

Varna
Bustling Varna is home to the **Aphrodite Beauty Spa and Health Clinic** at the Helios Spa & Resort. The resort is located within the ancient forest of the Golden Sands nature park close to the region's liveliest beaches. The spa offers a staggering array of traditional Bulgarian health treatments together with a range of holistic and contemporary well-being therapies. There are indoor pools, two saunas, a steam room, whirlpool, solarium and high-tech hydro-baths equipped with a wide variety of massage nozzles and 25 shades of light as part of a therapeutic built-in underwater illumination system. Spa-goers can select a hue to stimulate the senses and trigger positive healing emotions as intensive

massage jets caress and knead tension, stress and fatigue away.

St Konstantin
The picture-postcard resort of St Konstantin is one of the traditional spots on the Black Sea shoreline. Nestled among cypress palms and fig trees on a landscape dotted with healing mineral springs, St Konstantin comprises a mix of traditional spa hotels, vacation villas and holiday resorts.

The **Romance Spa**, within the Romance Splendid Hotel, is located in a picturesque national park famous for its mineral waters. This popular spring-fed spa centre has both outdoor and indoor mineralized pools, together with a hydro-massage bathtub, solarium and beauty suite. Guests are offered a highly personalized spa package designed to meet individual wellness needs using organic, ecologically sound products. Try the Vichy shower to experience the tantalizing massaging effect of warm water cascades on the body or aromatherapy massages, sauna and a host of body therapies that place relaxation to the fore.

GREECE

travel essentials

TIME ZONE: GMT+2

TELEPHONE CODE: +30

CURRENCY: Euro

CAPITAL: Athens

LANGUAGE: Greek

WHEN TO GO: A Mediterranean climate boasts plenty of sunshine and a limited amount of rainfall. Dry hot days in summer are cooled by seasonal winds (*meltemi*) but can still be stifling. Winters are generally mild in lowland areas, with a minimum amount of snow and ice.

Athens

In honour of the Greek ouzo tradition, the old-style Hotel Grande Bretagne in Athens has concocted a modern-day twist on the nation's ancient wellness rituals using the Grecian tipple.

ABOVE Anise is one of the herbs used in ouzo.

RIGHT Bastion of Grecian health therapies – the GB Spa.

OPPOSITE Pillars of the Parthenon, Athens.

PREVIOUS PAGE Imerovigli, Santorini (see page 144).

Since early Byzantine times, Greeks have believed that their potent national tipple, ouzo, has healing properties, extolling its medicinal benefits to such an extent that it was dubbed '*to farmako*' in health folklore – simply meaning 'the medicine'. Ouzo is a purely Greek concoction, made from alcohol extracted from raisins and blended with aromatic mountain herbs such as aniseed, coriander and amaranth.

An Old Remedy

During the Ottoman era, it was used as a sedative and soothing gastric cure; its subtle liquorice flavours diluted with water at a 4:1 ratio. Ouzo evokes nuts, herbs, flowers and anise and with an alcohol content of 40–80 per cent proof it packs a wallop in every sip. However, when blended with olive oil, it can be gently massaged into small cuts and abrasions as an antiseptic. It also provides a deep, calming scent and is gently purgative, with a few droplets

3 things you **must not** miss

◄ 1 Anafiotika
Lose yourself in the olden charms of the city's Anafiotika district. Wander among the pretty 19th-century stone-built homes. *www.visit greece.gr*

2 Step Back in Time
Absorb the grandeur of over 3,000 years of ancient history at the Acropolis, the Choregic Monument of Lysicrates and Filopappos (Hill of the Muses). *www.breathtakingathens.com*

3 Evening Out
Join the locals in a leisurely *volta* (stroll) through the lively main drags of the Plaka and Kolonaki Square; a sociable prelude to an evening in Athens' innumerable bars and restaurants.

effective as a digestif after a heavy meal. Older Greeks still swear by rubbing ouzo into tired muscles and aching joints – a very good reason why it is common in spa therapies intended to revive and restore.

Restorative and Rejuvenating

The **Hotel Grande Bretagne** offers breathtaking views of the famed Acropolis, the Parthenon and the original Olympic Stadium from a stylish, tranquil interior that pays homage to Greek culture. Spa therapies at the hotel's **GB Spa** fuse age-old Mediterranean health ideas with modern approaches. Their ouzo-oil massage is one of the capital's best-kept therapeutic secrets.

The healing properties of ouzo in this sumptuous touch therapy are activated by sensuous, rhythmic, deep strokes. Clear in colour, ouzo becomes milky white when mixed with water or ice, an effect of the anise oil when the alcohol is diluted. In oil form, anise has diuretic and oestrogenic qualities that can help to control weight, reduce flatulence and colic, ease menstrual pain and reduce cellulite. This deeply calming and aromatic touch therapy takes place among basalt stones, Greek statues and vases full of blooms, setting the tone for a transcendental experience devoted to pampering rejuvenation.

Other notable spas in Athens that offer all-natural therapies inspired by Greek culture include the sumptuous **Hotel Divani Apollon Palace & Spa** and the upmarket **Athens Park Hotel & Spa.**

RIGHT Pool at the GB Spa.

Greek Islands

In the Greek islands, which are renowned for their therapeutic spas, the tradition of olive-oil wellness therapies continues to thrive among pine-clad mountains, citrus groves and sparkling seas.

In Greek mythology, Minerva the virgin goddess of medicine exalted the olive for its tasty, health-giving fruits and nourishing oil that soothes wounds, softens skin and strengthens bones and muscles. Athena, the goddess of wisdom and peace, struck her magic spear into the earth and it turned into an olive tree – a sacred site that grew into Athens. Today, citizens of the capital still claim that all Greek olive trees originate from rooted cuttings grown from that original olive tree.

In Greece, the olive remains at the heart of Grecian natural medicine with each crop yielding its own individual curative character. Olive leaves are used in Bach flower remedies to treat physical and emotional exhaustion and the fragrant essence of the pretty creamy-white olive flower can be applied in a compress to lessen anxiety. Olive oil, cold pressed from the fruit, has long been thought to protect the digestive tract, lower bad cholesterol and keep the heart and arteries healthy. A diet rich in olives and olive oil is believed to help promote the growth of shiny hair, prevent dandruff, strengthen nails, prevent wrinkles, cancel out the effects of alcohol, soothe aching muscles and ease stiff joints.

The oil can also be rubbed into the skin to help keep it soft and supple. Rich in antioxidants, olive oil is packed with easily absorbable vitamin E, which is believed to be a natural defence against the signs of ageing. Olive husks are used to make a rich, nourishing soap while olive skins can enrich the health of the scalp when used as a healing, moisturizing emollient.

ABOVE Olive oil – nature's moisturizer.

Mykonos

On the historic island of Mykonos, the **Cavo Tagoo Spa** is drenched in Cycladean light, facing Delos, the birthplace of the mythical god of the sun, Apollo. Fusing a traditional Grecian approach to wellness

3 things you **must not** miss

1 Santorini's Past
Archaeology buffs will marvel at the relics of Thira, an ancient Dorian city with 9th-century BC tombs, Hellenistic houses and Byzantine fortifications. *www.visit greece.gr*

2 Crete's Natural Wonder
Relish the challenge of hiking the Samaria Gorge, the longest gorge in Europe. The hike takes around seven hours; read up about it before you go, to make sure you're up to it. *www.visitgreece.gr*

▶ **3 Sights of Mykonos**
Admire the old wooden windmills, and the island's Little Venice district, where 16th- and 17th-century buildings teeter on the shoreline, balconies over-spilling with blooms.

ABOVE *Oasis of calm – the Cavo Tagoo Spa.*

BELOW *Beautiful coastline of Mykonos.*

OPPOSITE *Soothing waters of Elounda Spa & Thalassotherapy.*

and beauty in an array of award-winning treatments and products, the Cavo Tagoo Spa transports guests on a journey through indigenous ingredients, such as coarse mineral-rich Aegean sea salt, Aegean seaweed extracts, lavender extract and locally grown sagebrush, herbs and roses. Using special blends of the spa's own signature olive oil, therapies ease the body into a state of calm relaxation as the aromatic effects help to balance mind, body and soul.

Crete

Therapies are similarly influenced by authentic Greek traditions at the **Elounda Spa and Thalassotherapy** at the Blue Palace Resort on the island of Crete, where a curative scrub for super-soft skin uses liberal quantities of home-made olive oil. Each therapeutic session is delivered beach-side, offering guests the finest, and oh-so-calming, views across the sea. Inspired by the everyday life of the ancient locals and the homespun Greek produce – such as mint, sage, eucalyptus, wild rose, yogurt, olive seeds and olive oils – the skin is purified, softened, smoothed, nourished and calmed.

CAVO TAGOO SPA

t +30 22890 20100
w www.cavotagoo.gr

*One of their signature
therapies, a 1-hour holistic
massage using olive oil,
costs €100 euros – truly
sublime.*

**ELOUNDA SPA AND
THALASSOTHERAPY,
BLUE PALACE RESORT**

t +30 2810 300330
w www.eloundahotels.co.uk

*Choose from rich olive-oil
massages and facials
infused with Cretan herbs
(from €60).*

**EUPHORIA WELLNESS
SPA, ALBATROS SPA
RESORT HOTEL**

t +30 28970 22144
w www.albatros.gr

*This spa offers a number of
different therapies using
oilve oil. A traditional olive-oil
massage lasting 25 minutes
costs €60*

**ROCABELLA RESORT
& SPA**

t +30 22860 23711
w www.rocabella-hotel-
  santorini.com

*Indulge in a sumptuous
mineral-water bath with olive
oil – the ultimate soothing
skin nourishment (€60).*

*RIGHT Luxuriant R&R at the
upscale Rocabella Resort
& Spa.*

Adding a few drops of raki – the potent traditional non-sweet, anise-flavoured Cretan spirit – to a traditional Cretan olive oil is believed to open up the senses. After an exfoliating face peel using the efficacious stones of the olive, the skin is ready for a generous slathering of the therapeutic elements of the island's golden-amber oil to achieve blissful serenity and body balance.

Though small in size, the **Euphoria Wellness Spa** at the Albatros Spa Resort Hotel in Hersonissos offers an intimate one-to-one programme of all-Greek rejuvenating treatments that reflect the fertile, health-giving local terrain. Therapies are created using all-natural essential oils, olive oil, Cretan red wine, Aegean algae, plants and therapeutic mineral spring water. Only the purest Cretan olive oil is used in the body-drenching hydration therapy: a richly nourishing wellness ritual that starts with a drizzle of Crete's self-proclaimed 'liquid gold'. Organically grown and traditionally produced from the first cold pressing of handpicked Koroneiki olives from the groves of the North Mylopotamos region, this utterly unforgettable deluge of the senses culminates in delectable full-body saturation to the sensual rhythm of syncopated, synchronized deep massage strokes.

Santorini

Located on the outskirts of Imerovigli, just 1.5km (1 mile) from the capital city Fira, the **Rocabella Resort & Spa** is famous for its timeless beauty. Against a magical Grecian backdrop of caldera views, sunsets sinking into Aegean waters, beaches surrounded by high volcanic-rock cliffs and traditional whitewashed houses, this well-appointed wellness centre stretches out towards the cliff side over 305m (1,000ft) above deep cobalt waters said to guard the lost city of Atlantis.

Renowned for its focus on pure, natural and environmentally friendly products, a diverse menu of Greek-inspired therapies has been designed to quench the needs of even the most demanding spa connoisseur. Enjoy a decadent massage outdoors at sunset, feeling the cooling breeze off the sea and watching as flickering candles add their glow to a crimson sky. In winter, you can take a hot bath in the many thermal-water outlets that are found in the small lava bays around the area's volcanic rim. Other on-site therapies use the finest botanical ingredients and produce of the island's landscape, from local pumice formed by sedimentary lava from the craggy slopes to virgin olive oil from thousand-year-old olive groves.

TURKEY

travel essentials

TIME ZONE: GMT +2

TELEPHONE CODE: +90

CURRENCY: New Turkish Lira

CAPITAL: Ankara

LANGUAGE: Turkish

WHEN TO GO: Western Anatolia offers average temperatures of 9°C (48°F) in winter and 29°C (84°F) in summer, while the snowy plateau regions can drop to winter averages of -2°C (28°F). On the Black Sea coast, a wet, warm and humid summer (23°C/73°F) and mild winters (7°C/45°F) contrasts with eastern Anatolia where harsh winters see snow cover from November until the end of April and temperatures of around -13°C (9°F).

Istanbul

Istanbul's bathing institutions remain an important part of the social fabric of the city, drawing diehard hammam-goers and travellers alike to the city's oh-so-famous, palatial bathhouses.

ABOVE Hammam at the Ritz-Carlton's Laveda Spa.

RIGHT Sultanahmet Camii; its more familiar name is the Blue Mosque.

OPPOSITE Atmopsheric bathing at the traditional Cağaloğlu Hamamı.

PREVIOUS PAGE View of Istanbul.

During the Roman Empire the resounding boom of a copper gong would fill the streets at dawn, heralding the opening of the baths. After the Ottoman Empire conquered Turkey in the 15th century the baths were even more popular, combining the Islamic obsession with personal cleanliness with the Greco-Roman tradition of public bathing. Today the hammams are used as a sanctuary from the hubbub of the city, and the grandest of all is the **Cağaloğlu Hamamı**.

Scrub, Cleanse and Steam

For many Turks the Cağaloğlu Hamamı, in among the elaborate domes, chaotic bazaars, cobblestone alleyways and gleaming minarets, represents the ancient social heart of Sultanahmet (Old Istanbul). Since 1741 this bathhouse has been a gathering place for the masses. Entering from a noisy side street, bath-goers arrive in

a grimy, city-weary state only to emerge two hours later revived, rosy-cheeked and thoroughly cleansed. Past visitors here form an eclectic roll-call: Florence Nightingale,

3 things you must not miss

◀ 1 Haggle in the Market
Haggle your way around the 4,000 stalls of the Kapalı Çarşı (Grand Bazaar), Turkey's largest covered market, for beautiful Turkish carpets, glazed tiles, pottery, copper, brassware and leather goods. *www.tourismturkey.org*

2 Cruise the Straits
Take a cruise along the mighty Asia-meets-Europe Bosporus Straits past many of the iconic sights of Istanbul. You can use the local ferry or many private operators run tours.

3 Sample Local Cuisine
Enjoy the rich flavours, fresh produce and age-old recipes (some with a modern touch) in this gastronomic city, where everything from a humble kebab and mezze to lavish roast lamb banquets are exceptionally tasty – and surprisingly cheap.

INFORMATION

CAĞALOĞLU HAMAMI

t +90 212 522 24 24
w www.cagaloglu
hamami.com.tr

Entrance to this old-style Turkish bath is just 25 YTL but for a basic package with a cleansing ritual you'll need to pay around double that. There is no need to pay for the full tourist deal, which is basically an inferior option at a higher price.

ÇEMBERLITAŞ HAMAMı

t +90 212 522 79 74
w www.cemberlitas
hamami.com.tr

A scrub, massage and wash by the attendant lasts for approximately 15 minutes. Entrance with bathing is 35 YTL, with massage 55 YTL.

SÜLEYMANIYE HAMAM

t + 90 212 519 55 69
w www.suleymaniye
hamami.com.tr

Probably the most luxurious of Istanbul's old-style traditional bathing experiences. Entrance and a 15-minute deep-cleansing is 70 YTL.

LAVEDA SPA, RITZ-CARLTON ISTANBUL

t +90 212 334 44 44
w www.ritzcarlton.com

Try the 45-minute luxurious steam-bath ritual for the ultimate Turkish-style splurge, priced at 160 YTL.

ABOVE *Bathing pool at the Laveda Spa.*

singer Tony Curtis and actors Omar Sharif and Harrison Ford, Formula 1's Jenson Button and rock star Brian May.

Most visitors opt for a set cleansing and bathing routine, choosing a wash and/or a massage from a small menu of options. After paying a fee, you undress and wrap yourself in a small cloth. Footwear is provided – either traditional wooden clogs or flip-flops.

First, you'll be encouraged to laze around on a heated marble slab in order to work up a gentle sweat. As the body perspires, dirt and toxins are loosened, necessitating a brisk scrub after 20 minutes with a loofah. Next you'll be stretched out face down on the marble for a thorough drenching with tepid water before being dried with a rough towel. A dry massage with a *kese* (a scratchy mitten) follows; this is a sandpaper-style exfoliation rub that turns every inch of skin bright pink. Now, the soap – and this is lather on a gigantic scale, worked up into frothy towers of bubbles using an enormous sponge. After cleansing every bodily nook and cranny (this is no time to be shy) and being subjected to some serious sluicing, you'll be massaged with oil (if you've chosen the de luxe option) or urged to allow your body

to cool down by relaxing around the baths. On a busy day, when the baths are packed, the noise can be infernal as similarly well-cleansed, shiny-skinned companions chat. However, most visitors will find the light-shafted, domed, cathedral-like interior strangely ethereal.

Other venues that capture the ambience of the bathing tradition include the **Çemberlitaş Hamamı** and the **Süleymaniye Hamam**.

Ottoman-inspired Decadence

Seeking a more lavish option with plenty of opulent five-star touches? Then consider the Ottoman-inspired splendour of the **Laveda Spa** at the Ritz-Carlton hotel on the banks of the mighty Bosporus. Here, stunning tilework draws on the city's architectural heritage. Characterized by elegant domes, columns, mosaics and vaulted ceilings, the hammam is a luxurious oasis of calm. While the rituals follow traditional lines, privacy is guaranteed. You're swathed in thick, fluffy towels and sumptuous velvety robes. Bowls of exotic fruits and glasses of spring water provide refreshment in the rug-strewn relaxation room where flickering candles and lilting spa melodies lull you into a post-hammam snooze.

Pamukkale

Pamukkale (meaning 'cotton castle') appears to be swathed in folds of diamond-encrusted velvet that gather in glittering drapes around the scenic foothills of the Cökelez Mountains.

ABOVE Ancient bas-relief at Hierapolis.

Adorned with step-terraced pools and stalactites on a hillside cliff of alabaster hues perched 200m (656ft) on top of a dramatic plateau, Pamukkale's stunning UNESCO-protected neon-white terrain dazzles with a generous frosting of Mother Nature's sparkle courtesy of a copious supply of carbonate minerals. Located in Turkey's south-west region, 22km (13½ miles) north of Denizli, Pamukkale boasts some of the most distinctive geological characteristics in the country.

Among natural-stone towers and once-gushing fossilized cascades, a spine of travertine peaks is home to a cluster of steam-shrouded crescent-shaped pools. With an average flow of 250 litres (55 gallons) per second at a constant temperature of 35°C (95°F), the waters of Pamukkale's snow-white lands originate from fissures between Mesozoic crystalline rocks and Neogene strata. Boasting a high content of calcium bicarbonate, the pools are tinged with a greenish glow and are characterized by natural weirs of water that spill over from a ridge of jaw-like dagger-shaped overhangs. A year-round constant dousing of fresh calcium carbonate coats the travertine waterfalls in a glittering cloak of dazzling white. Ancient boulders of crystalline marble and quartz date back to the Pliocene Epoch.

Hierapolis

Extending alongside the jaw-dropping resplendent ruins of the Greco-Roman-Byzantine town of Hierapolis (founded around the springs in the 2nd century BC), Pamukkale enjoys striking views across this ancient resort established by Greek king Attalus of Pergamon. The town has grand bathing venues, temples, colonnaded boulevards, amphitheatres and monuments. Earthquakes in years gone by

3 things you **must not** miss

1 Birdwatching

Attracting 203 different species of breeding birds, including flamingos and ducks, Çaltı (Beylerli) Lake (between Denizli and Dinar) is an important ornithology hangout. *www.pamukkale.net*

2 'Crying Rock'

Admire the astounding natural beauty of the Sakızcılar Asmaaltı Waterfall in Sakızcılar Village. The falls are located by the popular Hocanın Yeri picnic spot. *www.denizli.bel.tr*

▶ 3 National Park

Visit the flora-rich terrain of Mount Honaz National Park and Kartal Lake Pine Forest. *www.cevreorman.gov.tr*

have caused many of the buildings at the lowest end of the town to become embedded in travertine – to dramatic effect. With its temples and basilica, the resort became a Byzantine bishopric and place of Christian pilgrimage.

Pamukkale's Precious Waters

Pamukkale itself was relatively unknown until the 1960s when it was added to the hippie trail by both Turks and foreigners as a tranquil destination with a spiritual aura. Today it is a popular place to submerge in the healing waters, either in the natural pools on occasion or in purpose-built

RICHMOND PAMUKKALE
SPA

t +90 258 271 42 96

w www.richmond
hotels.com.tr

*The hotel's high-tech sauna,
steam room and indoor and
outdoor thermal pools are
free for guests' use.
Additional spa therapies
inspired by the geothermal
terrain are priced from
80 YTL.*

SPA HOTEL COLOSSAE
THERMAL

t +90 258 271 41 56

w www.colossaehotel.com

*Relax in a column-flanked
indoor thermal pool suite
under a domed glass atrium.
Three-, five- and seven-day
wellness programmes
tailored to weight loss, de-
stressing, anti-ageing and
relaxation are available. A
traditional Turkish bath
complete with scrub costs
around 65 YTL.*

PAM THERMAL HOTEL

t +90 258 271 41 40

w www.pamthermal.com

*Hotel guests can use the
thermal pool and therapeutic
whirlpool baths 24 hours a
day, year-round, for no extra
charge.*

*ABOVE Bubbling, hot, healing
springs, Pamukkale.*

bathing areas constructed to help alleviate problems with the degradation of this spectacular geological phenomenon. Environmental preservation has been at the forefront of activities in this ancient wellness zone set within an internationally designated Mediterranean Conservation Hotspot and WWF Global 200 Freshwater Eco-region. Declared a UNESCO site in 1992, visitors are now restricted to certain pathways (where you must walk barefoot) to maintain the exceptional quality of Pamukkale's travertine deposits.

Pamukkale retains its place in the heart and minds of Turks nationwide as the country's foremost mineral-bath spa because of its outstanding natural beauty and healing hot-water calcium-rich sacred springs. Expansive tombs scattered around the countryside remain synonymous with quiet meditation despite modern-day tourist development. Deep-rooted beliefs centre on the curative properties of these milk-white chalky waters, now much revered. As they bubble and splash down the snow-white limestone slopes across vibrant pink clumps of sprouting oleanders, Pamukkale's precious spring waters collect in basins, crevices and small hollows – some organically carved from the rock to form to delicate scallop-shell and petal shapes. Sporadic daubs of colour are added by a build-up of sulphur and iron oxide to add pockmarks of yellow, red and green over the frosted terrain. In cold weather, you can witness great rising columns of mist swirling over the landscape of this white 'castle' – Turkey's eye-popping mineral-crusted calcareous fairyland.

A steady stream of water-loving pilgrims schedule an annual therapeutic visit to Pamukkale's curative wonders. The pH of the water is around 6.0 and drinking and

bathing are both recommended for the possible positive effects on rheumatic aches, dermatological ailments, neurological and physical exhaustion and nutritional disorders.

Geothermal Pampering

Few settings are more recuperative than this bizarre tangle of radiant, dazzling solidified cascades, which are especially eye-catching when the travertine terraces and conglomerations of stalactites are struck by the golden rays of the sun. For added luxury, a number of well-appointed spa hotels have sprung up around Pamukkale to cater for hot-spring aficionados, from the ultra-swish 206-room **Richmond Pamukkale Spa** and 5-star 231-room **Spa Hotel Colossae Thermal** to 236-room comfy budget option the **Pam Thermal Hotel**. Most offer a programme of therapeutic packages centred very much on the local waters, with stress-reducing hydrotherapy massages and mineral-rich whirlpool baths a speciality for easing fatigue, aches and pains and reducing tension.

ENGLAND

travel essentials

TIME DIFFERENCE: GMT

TELEPHONE CODE: +44

CURRENCY: Pound sterling

CAPITAL: London

LANGUAGE: English

WHEN TO GO: Surrounding seas ensure England has a year-round temperate maritime climate with variable, unpredictable weather that can change from day to day. Winters are cool, while summers are warm, if wet. Temperatures rarely dip much below 0°C (32°F) or reach higher than 29°C (84°F), with stiff sea breezes around the coasts.

Lake District

The Lake District is, of course, inextricably linked with one natural resource – namely water. However of all the vast water expanses found in the region only one is actually a lake – Bassenthwaite.

ABOVE Outdoor hot tub, Armathwaite Hall Country House Hotel and Spa.

OPPOSITE ABOVE Bathing Pool at Armathwaite Hall Country House Hotel and Spa.

OPPOSITE BELOW View of tranquil shores of Bassenthwaite Lake.

PREVIOUS PAGE Thermae Bath Spa (see page 156).

Steeped in myths and legends, this peaceful water mass is the fourth-largest in the Lake District at 518ha (1,280 acres). Water in the Bassenthwaite area has been filtered through rocks dating back millions of years with much of it so pure it can be drunk straight from the ground. The tranquil shores of Bassenthwaite (a nature reserve and Special Area of Conservation) are surrounded by numerous underground springs and dozens of trickling streams.

Magic of Bassenthwaite

Drawn from deep in the beautiful Cumbrian countryside, the water is said to combine health-giving properties with a rich spirit, according to Lakeland lore. Water fairies could grant wishes, while the lakes themselves were believed to be magical gateways to the world of the gods. On the summer solstice the Mother of the Water (Water Goddess) is honoured at Bassenthwaite. Marked by a late Neolithic

stone circle, an almost perfect ring some 38m (125ft) in diameter, the powerful and mysterious charms of the 'Queen of the Deep' are said to represent the great ocean of our emotions.

The low-sodium, low-nitrate water is considered one of the highest-quality sources in the UK. Beautifully delicate on the skin and tantalizingly refreshing on the tongue, Lakeland spring water bubbles up amid reed beds, marshland, woodlands and wildflower meadows in a glacially-eroded valley set within a breathtakingly beautiful alluvial plain. Here in this stunning natural backdrop – described by *National Geographic* as one of the '50 places in the world to visit' – is also where you'll find the Lake District's finest water-side spa.

Lakeside Spa

With views overlooking resplendent Bassenthwaite Lake, **Armathwaite Hall Country House Hotel and Spa** is a 17th-

3 things you must not miss

◄ **1 Trout Fishing**
Trout fishing in Esthwaite Water in Hawkshead, the largest stocked lake in the north-west of England, offers renowned top-of-the-water action set amid breathtaking scenery. *www.hawkshead trout.com*

2 18 Holes
Enjoy a true test of golf at the 18-hole Workington Golf Club, established in 1893, on the region's coastal fringe. *www.workingtongolfclub.com*

3 Adrenalin Fix
Exhilarating activities (including quad-biking, clay pigeon shooting, archery and abseiling) can be experienced at Holmescales Farm, Cumbria's fast-paced outdoor activity centre. *www.holme scales.com*

century former stately home framed by the lush, green Lakeland fells. Family-run with that magical mix of warm friendliness and exacting professionalism, Armathwaite Hall epitomizes noble lakeside rest and relaxation with a stunning spa that takes its inspiration from the lakeside setting.

At its heart is the stunning infinity pool illuminated by soft mood lighting and completed by an indoor waterfall, while an outdoor hot tub boasts unbeatable views across gardens and out to Bassenthwaite. A stylish thermal zone contains a hydrotherapy pool, aromatherapy steam room, scented showers and sauna. The vast therapy menu offers a sumptuous choice of spa treatments, many of which have their origins in the natural organics of the Lake District's springs, rivers, lakes and wells.

Attentive, highly talented wellness technicians demonstrate a clear passion for their job and their environs, providing lots of background detail on the botanical content of unique signature treatments: such as the 60-minute Primordial Waters Sculpting Energising Massage (a deep-touch therapy with fluid, soothing movements to the sound of gentle rain and water); the decadent 90-minute Tranquil Lakes therapy (a luxurious

candlelit hydration treatment that involves fragrant oils in a whirlpool bath); and the ultimate Bassenthwaite Ritual (a 90-minute idyllic bathing experience that uses flowing water to caress and rejuvenate the skin complete with sensual aromatic therapies) – a deeply restorative experience that leaves the skin wonderfully soft and smooth.

Outside, a carefully created Sensory Garden inspired by Bassenthwaite Lake and the surrounding mountains continues the Armathwaite spa experience. This leafy, bloom-filled oasis mixes plant textures and contrasting landscapes with considerable skill to provide a peaceful sanctuary close to Bassenthwaite's mystical, magical shores.

INFORMATION

ARMATHWAITE HALL COUNTRY HOUSE HOTEL AND SPA
t +44 1768 776 551
w www.armathwaite-hall.com

Step though the door of this calming oasis of tranquillity to breathe in the serenity that prevails throughout the spa, from the gorgeous lake-facing relaxation terrace and peaceful Zen room to the de luxe therapy suites where first-rate staff perform restorative magic (60-minute Primordial Waters Sculpting Energising Massage, £80).

Bath

Blessed with delightfully warm, thermal waters, the city of Bath allows visitors to share in a spa-going tradition much as the Celts and Romans did over 2,000 years ago.

ABOVE Fine historic city of Bath.

OPPOSITE Beautifully restored Roman Baths.

Bath's spas are the most famous natural spas in the UK. The fine, spring-fed Roman Baths date back to between the 1st and 4th centuries AD. Water rises up at a constant temperature of 46.5°C (115.7°F) amid the original Roman paving, the Great Baths, the remains of the Temple of Minerva and the more recent King's Bath, which dates from the 12th century. While you cannot bathe at the Roman Baths, you can visit them. There is an admission fee, but free audio guides and guided tours are available.

By the early 1800s, Bath (known as 'Aquae Sulis' in Roman times) had become a wellness resort for the affluent and aristocratic, who came to wallow in the bubbling waters, which were considered to be a cure for many afflictions.

Spa With a View

Today, visitors flock to the magnificent **Thermae Bath Spa**. At this day spa you can relax in the Minerva Bath, with its massage jets, whirlpool and 'lazy river', experience a series of aroma steam rooms, revive your tired feet in footbaths or be drenched in the waterfall shower.

But the most spectacular part of the spa is the open-air rooftop pool, which offers magnificent views of the city and the surrounding countryside. A twilight bathing package is available, and this gives you the romantic opportunity to see the gradual change in light and atmosphere at sundown – with a glass of wine in hand.

As the shadows cast mystical shapes across the reflection of an ancient Roman cityscape on the waters, you can peruse a menu of water-based therapies. One of the most soothing therapies involves being cradled by a therapist in the warm, mineral-rich waters while having your body gently stretched through a series of flowing movements that blend massage and acupressure to achieve a deep state of relaxation – utter bliss.

3 things you **must not** miss

◀ 1 Explore the City
You can explore in a variety of ways – open-top bus tours, boat tours, historic walking tours and bike tours – to get a good look at the elegant streets and spectacular architecture. *www.visit bath.co.uk*

2 Picnic in the Park
Picnic among mature trees, curious squirrels, wild birds, flower beds and shrubberies at Sydney Gardens, Bath's oldest park. *www.visit bath.co.uk*

3 Foodies' Feast
Enjoy fine food in a city renowned for its staggering array of award-winning eateries, from gourmet restaurants to quaint tea rooms and cosy pubs. *www.visitbath.co.uk*

THERMAE BATH SPA

t +44 1225 331 234

w www.thermaebathspa.com

Entry to the spa costs £24 for two hours and £34 for four hours.

Special spa packages for tourists cost less than £60 and include entrance to the Roman Baths, a three-course lunch or champagne afternoon tea in the Pump Room and a two-hour spa session.

Therapies should be booked well in advance.

MACDONALD BATH SPA HOTEL

t +44 1225 444 424

w www.macdonald
   hotels.co.uk

Try the Refining Facial to perk up dull, lifeless skin to restore natural glow, improve skin tone and leave skin softer, smoother and more radiant, £40 for 45 minutes.

ABOVE Rooftop bathing at the Thermae Bath Spa.

RIGHT Spurting jets at the hydropool at the Macdonald Bath Spa Hotel.

Decadent R&R

As an alternative to the Thermae Spa, consider the healing waters of the de luxe **Macdonald Bath Spa Hotel**'s sumptuous spa, where a fine array of well-honed signature treatments have been exclusively created by Decléor to combine the best of Bath's spa traditions with ancient Celtic well-being secrets. Guests can enjoy decadent rest and relaxation wrapped in velvety bathrobes among the soft lights and fragrant aromatherapy candles of the spa's tranquil relaxation room. Natural products and sensuous pampering contribute to a holistic sense of wellness. For the ultimate skin pampering, book a quenching facial or treat yourself to an hour-long Relaxer Body Massage, which uses nourishing balm to de-stress, release built-up tension and coax skin into a healthy glow.

IRELAND

travel essentials

TIME ZONE: GMT

TELEPHONE CODE: +353

CURRENCY: Euro

CAPITAL: Dublin

LANGUAGE: Irish Gaelic

WHEN TO GO: Ireland's prevailing warm, moist Atlantic winds and temperate climate characterize a landscape lavished with rainfall. Mild winters lead to cool summers, with May to September the driest period. Short, wet, foggy days predominate from November to February.

County Galway

County Galway is renowned for its plenitude of water. Its landscape is filled with warm springs, slow-moving rivers, gurgling creeks and gushing streams, which are nourished by bountiful rain showers.

ABOVE *Seaweed bath at the Delphi Mountain Resort.*

OPPOSITE *Jacuzzi with a view at the Delphi Mountain Resort.*

PREVIOUS PAGE *Connemara.*

Located in the scenic west of Ireland, Galway is home to the nation's largest lake, Lough Corrib, together with a shoreline studded with picturesque wave-kissed isles, such as the Aran Islands and Inishbofin. Lush meadows and green pastures roll down towards fertile shoreline stretches that are rich in indigenous seaweeds and nutrient-laden marine mud. Water and the naturally harvested products of the sea have been important to Galway for generations – not just in cultural and economic terms, but also for health.

Water of Life

The marine plants and mountain-spring waters of Galway have formed the basis of numerous health elixirs for centuries, together with the much-loved local barley, whiskey and stout. Whiskey is still referred to as *uisce beatha* (water of life), a pint of frothy-topped Guinness (the 'Black Stuff') is considered by many to be the nation's holy water and freshly harvested Irish kelp (*Fucus serratus*) mixed with pure water from Galway's babbling mountain springs is the age-old secret of eternal youth.

Many of the county's finest spas draw upon the endemic botanicals and traditional remedies to offer a wide spectrum of unique wellness therapies. Irish skin is renowned for its soft, warm glow and elasticity, so facials rank high among the most popular treatments booked by international guests. Choose from seasonal therapies that nourish the skin with the antioxidant compounds of Guinness or cleanse the dermal layers with intensive barley scrubs. Some treatments blend the health and beauty benefits of Ireland's sudsy black stout with whiskey and Galway's natural-spring water to volumize hair, detoxify the body or soothe dry and inflamed skin.

3 things you **must not** miss

◀ 1 Cliff Walk
Enjoy a walk along the magnificent Cliffs of Moher – one of Ireland's most spectacular natural wonders. *www.cliffsofmoher.ie*

2 Island Boat Trip
Take a boat trip out to scenic Inishmore, the largest of the picturesque Aran Islands, located about 48km (30 miles) from the mouth of Galway Bay. *www.galwaytourist.com/tours/*

3 Spectator Sport
Join locals and tourists alike on the Salmon Weir Bridge, close to Galway Cathedral, during the summer to marvel at the shoals of salmon making their way up the Corrib River to spawn.

Mountain Escape

Set within 162ha (400 acres) of forest, the award-winning **Delphi Mountain Resort** in Connemara has a stunning, scenic location adjacent to one of the world's best surfing spots – Cross Beach. While decadent, all-natural wellness treatments aim to reduce the effects of stress, boost cell rehydration and leave guests feeling restored and reborn, an impressive array of relaxing pursuits and leisure and adventure activities gives energy levels a boost. Offering one of Ireland's best-conceived therapy menus that is much beloved by spa-goers, a visit to

Delphi is all about rewarding your mind, body and soul with the ultimate luxury – escape.

The nourishing seaweed baths use detoxifying, mineral-rich, locally harvested kelp. This salty algal drenching helps to aid the skin's natural water-holding reservoir in order to achieve a lasting youthful appearance and a blemish-free complexion.

Other notable Galway wellness sanctuaries include the water-side **Lough Rea Hotel & Spa** and Wellpark's super-smart **g hotel**: two well-respected advocates of fine hospitality with high-end spa therapies to match.

INFORMATION

DELPHI MOUNTAIN RESORT
t +353 95 42208
w www.delphimountain
resort.com

Gorgeous all-natural forest spa built from indigenous stone and wood. Half-day packages from €100.

LOUGH REA HOTEL & SPA
t +353 91 880088
w www.loughreahotel
andspa.com

Try a revitalizing 45-minute shoulder massage (€40) to loosen stiff muscles.

THE G HOTEL
t +353 91 865200
w www.theghotel.ie

At this uber-chic designer spa, complete with peaceful Zen Garden, expect to pay around €105 for the signature Skin-Brightener Facial.

ICELAND

travel essentials

TIME ZONE: GMT

TELEPHONE CODE: +354

CURRENCY: Iceland Krona

CAPITAL: Reykjavik

LANGUAGE: Icelandic

WHEN TO GO: Iceland enjoys a cool temperate ocean climate, thanks to the Gulf Stream, with average July temperatures around 12°C (54°F) and fairly mild winter conditions. Snow becomes rain in spring, but is rarely more than a shower. Peak season is the bright, crisps months of May and June.

Blue Lagoon

Spa-goers can have a truly surreal bathing experience at the famous Blue Lagoon – a unique wellness concept in rural splendour less than an hour from the urban melee of capital city, Reykjavik.

What makes the **Blue Lagoon** so rich in therapeutic terms is a unique mix of minerals, silica and algae. With proven anti-ageing and restorative benefits, the Blue Lagoon sits on around 6 million litres (1,319,815 gallons) of geothermal seawater that gurgles up in warm, brackish spouts at around 37–39°C (98–102°F). Naturally renewed every 40 hours, the composition of the water in this unique ecosystem on the Reykjanes Peninsula is unlike any other on the planet. It rises up from holes as deep as 2,000m (6,561ft) to create a natural and beautifully picturesque spa.

With each steamy splash, the mineral-laden water coats the dramatic black lava terrain with a bizarre white glaze. Huge waterfalls provide a pounding cascade into deep blue water enlivened by algae, and paths carved out of jagged molten rock lead down to a collection of steamy brackish pools.

Lagoon Treatments

Treatments take place in and around the lagoon itself, including outside in the open air. Every therapy uses the natural botanical produce of the local environment with in-water treatments conducted on specially designed wooden benches and massage mattresses. Few natural boosts are as reviving as weightless floating in the lagoon's mineral-rich waters, exposed to the natural elements and pure Icelandic air. Choose from deep flotation (an 8-hour sleep equivalent) and gentle rejuvenating lava-dust and clay massages to a nourishing circulation-boosting treatment in seawater hot tubs for two. All of the therapies are 100 per cent pure and chemical free.

Silica touch therapies are especially popular as they deep cleanse, reduce stress, ease muscle tension and soften the skin. Each treatment begins with a scrub to

ABOVE Unworldly geothermal waters at the Blue Lagoon.

OPPOSITE Reykjavik.

3 things you **must not** miss

1 Videy Island
Just a few minutes from the centre of the city by boat, Videy was inhabited until the 1940s. It is here that you can find Iceland's oldest surviving stone building together with a staggering variety of birdlife. *www.visitreykjavik.is*

2 Retail Therapy
Make the most of Reykjavik's excellent shopping at the Kringlan Shopping Mall and the flea markets, boutiques and craft stores in the downtown district of Laugavegur in the trendy Skólavödustígur area. *www.visitreykjavik.is*

▶ 3 Whale-watching
The main whale-watching season is from April to October, with tours departing from Reykjavik to all coastal areas of Iceland. *www.visit reykjavik.is*

BLUE LAGOON
t +354 420 8800
w www.bluelagoon.com

Expect to pay 6,000 ISK for a deeply relaxing 30-minute Blue Lagoon massage using sweet-smelling oils containing active ingredients from the lagoon's nutrient-rich environs.

RIGHT AND BELOW The Blue Lagoon is famous for its steam-shrouded, natural bathing pools.

OPPOSITE Gnarled, lava-strewn terrain edges the lagoon.

exfoliate before a generous covering of silica is applied to the body. After 20 minutes, the nourishing silica is removed and the body cleansed using the lagoon's mineral-rich waters. A relaxing massage follows, using organic oils extracted from plants grown in the lagoon environs, to leave the skin soft and supple with a healthy glow.

Similarly invigorating is the renewing full-body treatment using harvested lagoon mineral salts as a polish to remove dead skin cells and stimulate blood circulation, leaving the complexion clean and fresh.

Potent Natural Force

While the Blue Lagoon experience is about beautification and body pampering, the location and its powerful natural energy makes it more than that. For there is something utterly captivating about the landscape and the considerable force it has in healing the mind. Hundreds of stressed-out business executives and frazzled people at the end of their emotional tethers find great peace and understanding here among the lava fields. It can't make everything all right of course, but things can feel a whole lot better when the mind is calm, moods are balanced and mental equilibrium and harmony is restored. Worry lines fade, serenity returns and guests leave having achieved an overwhelming sense of well-being – no mean feat in the modern world.

SWEDEN

travel essentials

TIME ZONE: GMT +1

TELEPHONE CODE: +46

CURRENCY: Swedish krona

CAPITAL: Stockholm

LANGUAGE: Swedish

WHEN TO GO: Sweden enjoys a favourable climate with mild, changeable weather influenced by continental high pressure from the east. Sunshine brings hot days in summer and brightens cold winters. White nights (24-hour sunlight) characterize land within the Arctic Circle from late May until mid-July. Winter, however, sees daylight diminish to around 5½ hours a day in northern areas.

Varberg

Invigorated by the bracing, fresh aromatic sea spray of the North Sea, the town of Varberg is renowned throughout Sweden for its traditional spa treatments.

For most Swedes, the word 'Varberg' is inextricably linked with the restoration and recuperation of mind, body and soul; a place where physical and emotional strength are revived after the rigours of a bitterly cold winter. For almost 200 years this picturesque wellness town has attracted royalty and literati to its clothes-optional beaches, beautiful countryside, rugged cliff tops and family-friendly sands; all of which are just a short distance away from some fine, traditional spas.

A Bathing Tradition

Tourists begin arriving in late spring to soak up the iron-rich waters from the Svarte spring, which has been the mainstay of Varberg's wellness traditions since 1811. When the first baths were established in 1823 it was a simple venue designed to cater for a handful of clients. However, such was the uptake due to the arrival of steamship travellers on the newly introduced coastal route that a rebuild was required to add a dozen much-needed bath suites by 1860. Other health-resort amenities were upgraded and improved, with a second state-of-the-art open-air bathhouse building constructed in 1866. Offering the very best in endemic therapies using, among other things, seaweed, mineral waters, sea salt and mud, the new spa building contained 20 rooms for massage and sauna. After severe storm damage in 1902, a third open-air bathing complex was built and remains robustly intact to this day.

Over the years, Varberg has become more and more salubrious as the architecture has grown increasingly grand and exotic. Its roots are in the 19th century's fascination for romantic Moorish style, with plenty of telltale signs of Turkish bath culture.

ABOVE Treatments using seaweed are very popular in Varberg.

OPPOSITE Kallbadhuset (Bathhouse) in Varberg.

3 things you **must not** miss

1 Hit the Beach
Join beachcombers, windsurfers and birdwatchers at Apelvikens Beach. It is famous for being one of northern Europe's best places for kitesurfing. *www.marknad varberg.se*

2 Society Park
Enjoy a leisurely stroll through the town's 19th-century Socitetsparken (Society Park). This was a popular ritual with spa guests in years gone by, when concerts were staged by the spa's very own brass band. *www.marknad varberg.se*

▶ 3 Follow the Trails
Getterön's cliffs are a favourite place to walk with nature lovers. The cliff-top trails weave through a conservation area and offer stunning views. *www.lansstyrelsen.se/halland/amnen/Naturvard/naturum getteron/*

INFORMATION

. . . .

VARBERGS KURORT

t +46 340 62 98 00

w www.comwell.com

*Hotel guests can use the
seawater pool without
charge. A one-day spa
package, including sauna,
massage, Roman and
Turkish baths and a variety
of marine-inspired therapies
is from 550 kr.*

**VARBERGS STADSHOTELL
& ASIA SPA**

t +46 340 690 100

w www.varbergs
    stadshotell.com

*Indulge in a sublime 70-
minute luxurious
aromamassage after a
relaxing seaweed bath for a
truly memorable full body
therapy. Priced from 895 kr.*

HOTEL FREGATTEN

t +46 340 67 70 00

w www.cchotelfregatten.se

*Choose from a range of
health therapies and
massage styles in the on-
site wellness centre where a
45-minute marine wrap
using organic kelp and sea
salt costs from 520 kr.*

What the Town Has to Offer

Some of the top spa hotels with international
visitors combine first-class wellness therapies
with high-end guest accommodation, such
as the swish **Varbergs Kurort** located on Lilla
Apelvikens Beach. Classically furnished, this
beautiful historic building is equipped with a
stylishly converted modern spa facility
complete with seawater pools, sauna,
Roman bath, massage rooms, Turkish
hammam and yoga suite, all just a few steps
from a soft, sandy beach.

Other notable wellness facilities can be
found at the **Varbergs Stadshotell & Asia
Spa**, where 21st-century technology and
ancient Eastern health philosophies combine.
Therapies offered include Japanese washing,
qigong and Balinese massage.

In contrast, the **Hotel Fregatten** is 100
per cent Nordic in culture, atmosphere and
design. The on-site minimalist
Kurortsstaden's Spa and the Fregatten
Atletica gym are havens of classic
Scandinavian health therapies including
saunas, massages and facial treatments.

All of these spa hotels have easy access
to Varberg's main attractions, including the
Brunnsparken (Well Park); the
Varmbadhuset (Hot Baths), where a 32°C
(90°F) saltwater pool helps to soothe aches
and pains; the town's elegant seafront
promenade; the Kallbadhuset (Open-air
Baths); and the lush, green, flower-filled
Societsparken (Society Park). Numerous
fitness, health-care, nutrition and organic-
foodstuff businesses have sprung up in and
around the town, ensuring everyone leaves
Varberg chilled out and considerably
healthier than when they arrived.

*ABOVE AND RIGHT Varbergs
Kurort.*

FINLAND

travel essentials

TIME DIFFERENCE: GMT +2

TELEPHONE CODE: +358

CURRENCY: Euro

CAPITAL: Helsinki

LANGUAGE: Finnish

WHEN TO GO: Bright spring months lead to magical summers of long light-filled days as city-dwellers retreat to the country en masse.
September–November is when Finland starts to prepare for winter, while December–February is snowy and icy although rarely without some sunshine.

Saariselkä

Within Finland's frosted Arctic landscape against a backdrop of glittering, crystallized icy peaks the Igloo Village at the Hotel Kakslauttanen in Saariselkä is a cold-climate-lover's delight.

ABOVE Icy dips are popular in Finland.

BELOW Traditional smoke sauna, Hotel Kakslauttanen.

OPPOSITE Glass igloos at Hotel Kakslauttanen.

PREVIOUS PAGE Northern Lights.

Shrouded in a shimmering flurry of snowflakes on an alabaster snow-crusted carpet, this is Finnish igloo chic at its finest. Epitomizing a wintery wonderland offering untold snowy splendour complete with frosted gullies and dramatic icescapes, the **Hotel Kakslauttanen** offers guests a chance to stay in either a traditional ice-hewn or glass igloo in their Igloo Village. Having sheltered travellers for hundreds of years, Finland's arctic snow shelters now have some luxurious touches yet retain the old character of Lapland's dome-shaped ice-houses.

Keeping Out the Cold

Served by Ivalo airport, the Igloo Village opens each year from December/January – when temperatures settle between 0° and -5°C (32° and 23°F) – to April. To stay here is to enjoy a smoke-fired sauna, a roll in the snow and an ice massage under a star-scattered sky before being wrapped in a feather-filled sleeping bag and sipping a hot-chocolate nightcap.

The temperature inside the snow igloo stays between -3° and -6°C (27° and 21°F). Besides a sleeping bag, you are given woollen socks and a hood.

In the region's 'warmer' months, accommodation is in rustic wooden cabins, each with a private sauna and stunning scenic views.

3 things you **must not** miss

◀ 1 Birdwatching
In summertime in the fell tops and riversides along the wildlife-rich Iisakkipää nature trail you can spot an array of Arctic and migratory species, such as the Siberian tit (*Parus cinctus*, shown left). *www.visit finland.com*

2 Cross-country Skiing
Cross-country skiing in the Urho Kekkonen National Park is across a snowy paradise of well-maintained tracks conveniently punctuated by several coffee pit stops and rustic cafes. *www.outdoors.fi*

3 Snowmobile Rides
Take a white-knuckle snowmobile ride along tracks maintained by the Finnish Forest and Park Service authorities. The tracks are accurately waymarked by round, blue signs. *www. metsa.fi*

INFORMATION

• • • • • • • • • • • • • •

**HOTEL
KAKSLAUTTANEN**
t +358 16 667 100
w www.kakslauttanen.fi

*Embracing the wellness
benefits of fresh, pure Arctic
air, a spectacular snowy
landscape and sub-zero
temperatures, the Igloo
Village is dedicated to
Finnish-style leisure and
relaxation. Guests can use
the traditional smoke sauna
and ice pool at no extra
charge (it is around €300
per night to stay in an igloo).*

*ABOVE Cosy snow igloos at
Hotel Kakslauttanen.*

Health Benefits

In winter, Kakslauttanen takes the term 'chilling out' to a whole new level, when guests are encouraged to take a courageous curative dip in the surrounding gin-clear icy pools. The locals say that jumping into an ice-encrusted lake keeps you athletic, youthful and toned, with a good complexion and lots of energy.

The Finns swear by the health benefits of regular exposure to cold water citing it as an immune-boosting, natural high rich in endorphins that helps beat depression, opens the capillaries, veins and arteries and exfoliates the skin and rids it of toxins. Cold-water plunges are also believed to send the production of testosterone and oestrogen

soaring in men and women respectively. In addition to enhancing libido in both sexes, these hormones also play an important role in fertility. Swimming in cold water also burns up calories at a faster-than-normal rate.

Kakslauttanen's Igloo Village is also home to the world's largest smoke sauna, which overlooks the sparkling ice-topped waters of a pond. With enough room for 100 people, the sauna has a large 'cooling off' terrace and a nearby ice hole for the ultimate full-body icy immersion. If you're lucky, you'll then be soothed by the atmospheric dazzling magnificence of the Northern Lights, as the sky fills with vivid illuminations and the air with soft curative aromas of wafting honey-scented smoke.

Tampere

Though neighbouring Estonia boasts a lengthy sauna tradition, Finland is the undisputed sauna capital of the world. The town of Tampere is the home of Finland's oldest active public sauna.

Finland's third-largest city, Tampere, is located on the shore of Lake Näsijärvi, some 170km (106 miles) north of Helsinki. Almost 25 per cent of the terrain is water, with 180 lakes in the city area.

A Finnish Tradition

The word 'sauna' is borrowed straight from the Finnish word for the practice of trapping steam or heat in a confined area. Historically, public saunas were used by the poorest folk who didn't have their own sauna at home. Used for health purposes for well over 1,000 years, the sauna remains an intrinsic part of Finland's culture, with people visiting a sauna once or twice a week on average. Old-style saunas, such as the **Rajaportin Sauna**, have been used for a variety of health, relaxation and social purposes: childbirth (the heat is said to ease pain), preparing the dead for burial and as a place to knit and weave in the winter. When Finns are sick, they take a sauna and when children have a cold the sauna is the first port of call. Indeed an old Finnish proverb states: *Jos ei sauna ja viina ja terva auta niin se tauti on kuolemaksi;* meaning that if a sauna, whisky and tar salve don't make you well, death is imminent.

Authentic Sauna Experience

Built in 1906, the Rajaportin Sauna is now owned by the city and is run by the local sauna association in a traditional manner. This came about because the local authorities had threatened to tear the crumbling building down, but the Tampere sauna community fought hard to keep it open.

Rustic in design, the Rajaportin Sauna is is famous for its ultra-powerful sauna stove moulded into the rough, stone wall. Heated until crimson using a pile of burning logs, the stove pumps out a fearsome heat to reach around 95°C (203°F). Although this

3 things you must not miss

1 Flora and Fauna
Explore the nearby natural splendour of the Pirkanmaa region, where a wealth of Finnish flora and fauna can be enjoyed at the magnificent Helvetinjärvi National Park. *www.outdoors.fi*

2 Spy Museum
Marvel at the gadgets, gizmos and espionage secrets of Tampere's Vakoilumuseo (Spy Museum), the world's first according to the locals. *www.vakoilumuseo.fi*

▶ 3 Holiday Island
Revel in the great outdoors at the nearby Lomasaari Marttinen (Marttinen Holiday Island) in Virrat, where many activities and sports are on offer. *www.marttinen.fi* and *www.finland-tourism.com*

may seem like a punishment to the newbie, regular users are entirely comfortable with excessive sweating, cooling down intermittently using battered red buckets of water before repeating the cycle to stimulate the pores and cells. Separate seating for men and women is reached via a ramshackle staircase.

As a finale to the sweat-drenching experience, sauna-goers head to the benches outside to make the most of the cooling winter ice and snow.

For a plusher option with fluffy towels, slippers and showers, consider the **Scandic Tampere City** hotel.

ABOVE The unassuming
entrance to the Rajaportin
Sauna.

RIGHT Colourful wooden
houses in Pispala, the district
of Tampere that the Rajaportin
Sauna is located in.

TOURIST INFORMATION WEBSITES

Austria www.austria.info

Bulgaria www.bulgariatravel.org

Croatia www.croatia.hr

Czech Republic www.czechtourism.com

Estonia www.visitestonia.com

Finland www.visitfinland.com

France www.francetourism.com

Germany www.germany-tourism.de

Greece www.gnto.gr

Hungary www.budapestinfo.hu

Iceland www.visiticeland.com

Ireland www.visitbritain.com

Italy www.italiantourism.com

Latvia www.latvia.travel

Lithuania www.visitlithuania.net

Montenegro www.visit-montenegro.com

Poland www.poland.travel

Romania www.romaniatourism.com

Russia www.visitrussia.org.uk

Serbia www.serbia.travel

Slovakia www.slovakia.travel

Slovenia www.slovenia.info

Spain www.spain.info

Sweden www.visitsweden.com

Switzerland www.myswitzerland.com

Turkey www.tourismturkey.org

United Kingdom www.visitbritain.com

PICTURE CREDITS

Front Cover: **Tschuggen Grand Hotel and Bergoase Spa**; Back Cover: **Elin B @ Nordic Touch** (www.nordic touch.co.uk) left; **Blue Palace Resort and Spa, Elounda** centre; **Alamy/Gavin Hellier** right; **Aileen's Pics:** p.35; **Aire de Sevilla:** pp.12 top left, 13; **Alamy:** pp.10 (Sabine Lubenow), 17 (Jeronimo Alba), 20 (Jaubert Images), 28 (Mirko Angeli), 30 (Adam Eastland), 43 (David Sanger Photography), 47 (Alflo Co.Ltd), 49 (Prisma Bildagentur AG), 51 (INSADCO Photography), 56 (Danita Delimont), 57 (Profimedia International s.r.o), 59 (Jon Arnold), 65 (Profimedia International s.r.o.), 67 top left (Greg Balfour Evans), 69 (Profimedia International s.r.o.), 72 (Maciej Wotkowiak), 77 (Pegaz), 88 bottom left (TVeermae_Tallinn_Estonia), 92 (RIA Novosti), 121 (Diomedia), 122 (PCL),

147 (Gavin Hellier), 154 bottom left (Robert Read); **Alaskan Dude:** p.12 bottom right; **AlterdiMaggio1957:** p.29 bottom right; **Amber SPA Boutique Hotel:** p.84; **ANA Hotels:** p.128; **Aaron.Bihari:** p.156 top left; **Armathwaite Hall Country House and Spa:** pp.145 top left, 155; **Steve Arnold:** p.67 bottom left; **Arpingstone:** p.159 bottom left; **Axel-D:** p.64 top right; **Kaspar Bams:** p.123 top right, 124; **Bobak Ha'Eri:** p.63 bottom right; **Nick Bramhall:** p.29 top right; **Cavoo Tagoo Hotel:** p.142 top left; **Château Smith Haut Lafitte:** p.23; **Comwell Varbergs Kurort:** pp.167 top, 168; **Chursächsischen Veranstaltungs GmbH Bad Elster:** p.40, 41; **Simon Cole:** pp.163 top right, 164 bottom left; **Corbis:** pp.170 (Diane Cook and Len Jenshel), 171 (Anna Watson); **Danubius Health Spa and Resort Hévíz:** pp. 100 top left, 101 top right; **Danubius Health Spa and Resort Nove Lazne:** pp.3 top left, 62; **Danubius Spa and Resort Thermia:** p.68; **Delphi Mountain Resort:** pp.160 top, 161; **Druskininkai Tourism:** pp.79 , 80, 81; **Elin B @ Nordic Touch (www.nordic touch.co.uk):** pp.1, 98; **Estormiz:** p.170 bottom left; **Falkensteiner Hotels and Residences:** p.109 top right; **Finca Cortesin:** pp.15 top right, 16; **Finnish Tourist Board:** pp.169, 170 top left; **Dr. Dirk Förger:** p.131 bottom right; **Four Seasons Hotels and Resorts:** pp.24 bottom left (Barbara Craft), 25 (Barbara Craft); **FRED:** p.19 bottom right; © Anthony Georgieff; **Vagabond Media:** pp.6, 133, 134; **German National Tourist Board:** pp.42 bottom left, 45 top right & bottom right; **Grand Hotel Donat:** p.104; **Grand Hotel Pomerie-Balneo, SPA and Wellness:** p.135 top right; **Heiltherme Bad Watersdorf:** pp.55 top right, 60 top; **Hotel Hubertus:** p.50; **Hotel Kakslautten:** pp.170 bottom centre, 172; **Hungarian National Tourist Board:** pp.96 bottom left, 99; **Institute Igalo:** pp.117 top right, 118 bottom; **Images from Bulgaria:** pp.131 top right, 132, 135; **Istockphoto:** pp. 7 (Burcin Tuncer), 8 (Jaroslaw Grudzinski), 11 (Sergey Borisov), 14 (ArnauDesign), 18 (Andreas Karelias), 22 bottom left (Gregvr8156), 27 (Anssi Ruuska), 31 top right (Pacaypalla), 31 bottom right (Romaoslo), 32 (Brzozowska), 33 (Piero Malaer), 34 top right (Ingma Wesemann), 34 bottom right (Roland Zihlmann), 39 (x-drew), (42 top right (Qusek), 46 (DonStock), 48 top left (Todd Taulman), 52 top left (Kevin Klöpper), 53 (Dundanim), 62 (isifa Image Service s.r.o), 70 (Michal Krakowiak), 71 top left (Lord Runar), 73 top left (Blende64), 74 (Ffolas), 75 top left (Luke Daniek), 82 (Claudia Dewald), 83 top right (Dainis Derics), 83 bottom right (Andrei Männik), 85 (Anthony Rosenberg), 86 top left, (ferrantraite), 86 bottom left (Adrian Beeley), 87 (Andrei Nekrassov), 89 (LP7), 90 top left (Leon Rafael), 91 (Alexander Potapov), 93 top right (Mikhail Pogosov), 93 bottom right (Enrico Fianchini), 94 (Mikhail Pogosov), 95 (Pavlo Maydikov), 96 top left (Adam Mandoki), 100 bottom left (Hedda Gjerpen), 101 bottom right (Richard Schmidt-Zuper), 108 (Hrvoje Tomic), 109 bottom right (Ugurhan Betin), 110 (Neil Harrison), 117 bottom right (Dejan Suc), 118 top right (Michal Krakowiak), 119 top right (Nataliia Fedori), 119 bottom right (Danijela Pavlovic Markovic), 120 (Nataliia Fedori), 126 top left (Catherine Yeulet), 130 (Jivko Kazakov), 136 (Francesco Carucci), 137 (mbbirdy),

138 top left (esolia), 138 bottom left (Domenico Pellegriti), 139 (Ian Poole), 141 (Maria Toutoudaki), 142 bottom (Dieter Hawlan), 145 (Dominicus Antonius Franciscus Rijnart), 151 top (Luke Daniek), 149 top right (Syagci), 149 bottom right (Kazim Capaci), 150 (Pasticcio), 152 (Syagci), 159 (Przemyslaw Kilanowski), 160 bottom (Manuela Weschke), 162 (HannamariaH), 166 (David Elderfield), 174 (Aarre Rinne); **Kalma Saun:** pp.88 top right; **Klaus Nahr:** p.61 top right; **Janos Korom:** pp.103 bottom right, 106 bottom right; **Krusevac Tourism:** pp.114 top left, 115; **KUMerkle:** p.55 bottom right; **The Lavender Museum:** p.26; **Les Sources de Caudalie:** p.22 top left; **Jim Linwood:** p.63 top right; **Lipton Sale:** p.3 top right, 164 bottom left; **MacDonald Bath Spa Hotel:** pp.158 bottom right; **Martinnen:** p.173 bottom right; **Wolfgangus Mozart:** p.167 bottom; © **Museo Picasso Malaga:** p.15 bottom right (Bleda y Rosa); **National Tourism Organisation of Serbia:** pp.112, 113 (Dragan Bosnic), 114 bottom right; **Ocna Sibiului Spa:** p.127; **Alex Pnoiu:** p.128; **Park Hotel Richmond:** p.58 top left; **Photolibrary:** pp.19 top right (Pixtal Images), 21 (Hemis), 44, 78 (Wojteck Buss), 125 (Francesco Tomasinelli), 129, 157 (Steve Vilder), 16; **Pibwl:** p.71 bottom left; **Polish Tourist Board:** p.73; **Quinn Dombrowkski:** p.90 bottom left; **r h:** p.163 bottom right; **Rajaportin Sauna:** pp.173 top right, 174 top centre; **Ritz-Carlton Hotel Company:** p.146 top left, 148; **Rocabella Resort & Spa Santorini:** pp. 2,144; **Romania National Tourist Office:** p.123 bottom right; **Sacher Hotel, Wien:** p.54; **Shutterstock:** pp.61 bottom left (Pavel Kosek), 97 (Jule Berlin), 126 bottom left (Andrei Badau); **Slovenian Tourist Board:** pp.66 (Pepiccino), 103 top right, 102 &105 (Damijan MERC), 106 top right, 107 (D.Mladenovic), 166 (Mikhail Markoviskiy); **Softeis:** 48 bottom left; **Spa Vilnius Group:** p. 79, 80, 81 top right; **Starwood Hotels & Resorts Worldwide:** pp.138 centre right, 140, 143; **Sterol.Andro:** p.151 bottom right; **Stock Xchng:** pp.24 top right (Lize Rixt), 146 bottom left; **Swiss-image.ch:** p.33 (Lucia Degonda); **Thermae Bath Spa:** p.158 top (Andy Short); **Therme Vals:** p.38; **Jonathan White:** p.52 bottom left; **Wieliczka Salt Mine (www.kopalnia.eu):** p.76; **Russell Yarwood:** p.75 bottom left; **Zipacna1:** p.58 bottom left.

CAPTIONS

JACKET, FRONT COVER: Bergoase Spa at the Tschuggen Grand Hotel, Arosa.

JACKET, BACK COVER: (left) Széchenyi Baths, Budapest; (centre) Blue Palace Spa Elounda, Crete; (right) Cagaloglu Hamamı, Istanbul.

Pg 1: Széchenyi Baths, Budapest.

Pg 2: Rocabella Resort & Spa, Santorini.

Pg 3: (left) Danubius Health Spa Resort Nové Lázné, Mariánské Lázne; (right) Blue Lagoon, Iceland.

First published in 2011
by New Holland Publishers (UK) Ltd
London • Cape Town • Sydney • Auckland

www.newhollandpublishers.com

Garfield House, 86–88 Edgware Road,
London W2 2EA, United Kingdom

80 McKenzie Street, Cape Town 8001,
South Africa

Unit 1, 66 Gibbes Street, Chatswood,
NSW 2067, Australia

218 Lake Road, Northcote, Auckland,
New Zealand

Copyright © 2011 New Holland Publishers (UK) Ltd
Copyright © 2011 in text: Sarah Woods

10 9 8 7 6 5 4 3 2 1

ISBN 978 1 84773 818 9

Publisher: Guy Hobbs
Project editor: Clare Hubbard
Designer: Isobel Gillan
Picture research: Susannah Jayes
Cartography: Stephen Dew
Production: Marion Storz

Reproduction by Modern Age Repro House Ltd,
Hong Kong
Printed and bound by Tien Wah Press (Pte) Ltd,
Singapore

Although the publishers have made every effort to ensure that information contained in this book was researched and correct at the time of going to press, they accept no responsibility for any inaccuracies, loss, injury or inconvenience sustained by any person using this book as reference.